$\frac{P}{7}27$
$K37$
1993

FRAGMENTATION AND CONSENSUS

POLITICAL ORGANIZATION
AND THE INTERWAR CRISIS IN EUROPE

BY
LAURI KARVONEN

SOCIAL SCIENCE MONOGRAPHS, BOULDER
DISTRIBUTED BY COLUMBIA UNIVERSITY PRESS, NEW YORK

1993

Contents

Acknowledgments

This book was written while I spent my sabbatical at the University of Bergen, Norway. To be a guest of both the Department of Comparative Politics and the Norwegian Social Science Data Services (NSD) was a highly stimulating and altogether pleasant experience. My thanks really go to the staffs of these institutions *in corpore*. Special thanks are due to Björn Henrichsen, Stein Kuhnle, Jostein Ryssevik, Lars Holm, Anne Dueland, Bjarne Öymyr, Ulf Lindström, Frank Aarebrot, Pål Bakka, Terje Sande and Atle Alvheim. 'It was a very good year'.

I would not have started on this research had it not been for my participation in the project 'Crisis, Compromise and Collapse - Conditions of Democracy in Inter-War Europe' led by Dirk Berg-Schlosser of the Philipps University at Marburg. Portions of this manuscript have been presented and discussed in this group, and it is my pleasure to thank all participants in this ambitious and exciting research enterprise for a valuable exchange. My special thanks go to Ekkart Zimmermann previously of the University of the Bundeswehr, now of the Dresden Technical University.

Aleksander Loit of the Centre for Baltic Studies at the University of Stockholm provided essential data on Latvia, John F.N. Bradley on Czechoslovakia. John D. Stephens clarified an important point concerning Chapter 3. All of this is gratefully acknowledged.

Once again, the Social Science Commission of the Academy of Finland made it possible for me to do research on a full-time basis. Moreover, a 'Nordic Mobility Scholarship' from the Nordic Academy of Research (*Nordisk Forskarakademi, NorFA*) covered many of the extra expenses doing research abroad always entails.

The patience and understanding of my family while I was away from home was essential to the success of my work. Susan, Malin and Sven have, more than anyone else, earned my gratitude for making this project possible.

Hus Lindman
Åbo
January 1993   *Lauri Karvonen*

EUROPE AROUND 1938

Democracies

Repeated coups d'etat,
incomplete democratic rule

Democracies which collapsed
before the great depression

Democracies which collapsed
in the 1930s

Estonia 1934

Latvia 1934

Lithuania 1926

Poland 1926

Germany 1933

Austria 1933

Italy 1922

NORWEGIAN SOCIAL SCIENCE DATA SERVICES

Chapter 1

Introduction:
Two Theoretical Perspectives

This study deals with the fate of European democracy in the period between the two World Wars. Post-Versailles Europe entertained high hopes about a universal democratization of the continent; the coming two decades were to prove that Europe was still far from 'safe for democracy'. Why was it that democratic institutions remained (more or less) intact in some countries, while they succumbed to various authoritarian pressures in many others? This is the basic query which this book addresses.

The interwar period entailed the first general crisis of European democracy. It is quite natural that historians and social scientists have devoted considerable energies to uncovering the processes and mechanisms behind the outcome of the crisis. Without attempting to summarize the wealth of previous research one may simply note that the explanations and theories offered in the literature range from the most idiosyncratic analyses emphasizing the unique role played by individuals to grand schemes based on overarching social, economic and historical structures. While we should not yield to the idea that the beauty in social sciences is in the eye of the beholder, this variety of approaches and theories demonstrates that the crisis of interwar European democracy was indeed a multifaceted phenomenon which can be studied from numerous different angles.[1]

This study is guided by two general assumptions about the nature of the interwar crisis. First, the character of the crisis as a *general European phenomenon* is emphasized. To be sure, both the process of the crisis and its outcome display considerable variation from country to country. Still, no country can characterize this period as 'business as usual' from the point of

---

[1]. For those interested in explanations based on other factors than the ones stressed in this book, the most valuable sources will be Lipset 1981, Linz 1978, Luebbert 1991 and Stephens 1989.

view of its democratic institutions. Consequently, if one wishes to say something about this general phenomenon, a *comparative* perspective is called for; both countries where democracy survived the crisis and democracies that went under must be included in the study. Only this kind of an approach helps us determine the critical factors which go to explain the basic dynamics of the period.

Second, this study stresses the fact that the fate of political systems is a question of *political* nature. No matter what the ultimate 'causes' underlying the process may be, the chain of actions and reactions leading to the survival or dissolution of democratic practices and institutions involve political decisions on the part of political actors. Historical, economic, social and cultural structures and circumstances may strongly affect these decisions. Still they at best constitute a framework within which it is more or less likely that democracy may continue to function; they in themselves do not make decisions leading to the survival or demise of the political order.

The focus of the present research is on factors which were closely connected with the political organization of European countries in the interwar period. While not denying the importance of economic factors and social structures for the varying political outcomes across the continent, one is struck by the relative lack of cross-national efforts to determine the significance of more clearly political factors in this context.

Now, what is meant by 'political factors' is of course far from self-evident. In fact it could be argued that, for instance, most historical case studies are strongly involved in the use of political explanations, as their focus usually is on political elites and processes. Similarly, those researchers who emphasize the role of the ideological and philosophical foundations of politics may argue that their mode of explanation is of a political nature. In this study, however, 'political factors' means neither the tactical and strategic moves of the involved actors, nor the ideological side of politics. Rather, the focus is on more permanent aspects of politics: factors related to *party systems* and the way in which these condition the working of the democratic system are at the center of attention. At the theoretical level, the objective is to empirically test two contrasting theoretical notions concerning the functioning of party systems: assertions pertaining to the *fragmentation* of party systems, and the literature that goes under the heading of *consociationalism*. These two theories will be illuminated empirically in the two main empirical parts of the book. The premises and operational applications of these theories will be discussed more thoroughly in these parts of the study. Below, the essential features of these theories will be presented in a succint form in order to give the reader an introduction to the basic theoretical sphere of the book. The present chapter is concluded by a discussion of the aim and structure of the book.

Fragmentation

The question about the relationship between party systems and political stablity is a classic one in political science. In fact, it was first brought up at the end of the 19th Century, well before the breakthrough of mass democracy in Europe. In an analysis of 'Governments and Parties in Continental Europe', A. Lawrence Lowell argued that stable governments must have a majority of the Parliament behind them and consist of one party only. According to him, any coalition cabinet was faced with the task of pleasing a number of 'discordant groups' which necessarily rendered this kind of a cabinet more unstable. Similarly, Lawrence argued that stable government also required that the opposition consist of one party only; once the opposition had acquired a majority of the seats, it was to be able to form a one-party cabinet. The logical consequence of these propositions was that a two-party system was to be preferred to a multiparty system (quoted in Taylor and Herman 1971, 28).

This proposition was frequently cited in the political science literature of the early 20th century. Its rise to prominence did not, however, occur until after the second world war. Largely influenced by empirical observations about interwar European politics, above all the fate of democracy in Weimar Germany, F.A. Hermens in several works (1941, 1951, 1958) argued for the proposition that multiparty systems were inherently more unstable than two-party systems. According to Hermens, if one wished to etablish a strong and stable democracy, it was necessary to construct the party system so as to avoid the innate weaknesses of the multiparty system. This link between party system characteristics and democratic stability was, however, secondary in his argumentation. Instead, his name was to become associated with something of a crusade against *proportional representation*, which he believed to be the cause of the 'degeneration' of democracy into a multiparty system. By the same token, proportional representation allowed anti-system parties to gain seats in representative assemblies, thus further enfeebling the democratic institutions. In short, the type of electoral system determined the type of party system which in turn determined the stability of the democratic system. Lawrence Mayer (1989, 150) depicts Hermens' implicit causal model in the following manner (Figure 1).

Figure 1. F.A. Hermens' implicit causal model.

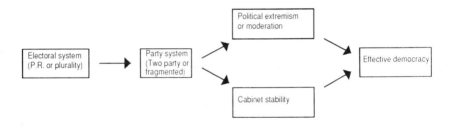

Reprinted with the permission of SAGE Publications, Inc.

Hermens influenced the scholarly debate of the first postwar decades to a large extent. Among others, such prominent scholars as V.O. Key (1959, 229-230), Anthony Downs (1957, 123-124) and Maurice Duverger (1951) argued much along the same lines as Hermens, albeit perhaps in a less definite manner. Duverger for one noted the correlation between proportional representation and multipartism (p. 281), the fact that those countries where fascism had succeeded had had electoral systems based on proportional representation (p. 286) as well as the observation that 'le multipartisme affaiblit le gouvernement parlementaire' (p.477).

All these authors, Hermens in particular, stressed the explanatory power of the electoral system. Proportional representation was the independent variable, whereas both party system fragmentation and the rise of anti-democratic groups were just steps on the way toward the breakdown of democracy. Consequently, it was the effect of the electoral system on the party system that became the main bone of contention in the ensuing scholarly debate. Here, it was soon found that Hermens had picked the empirical cases to suit his basic argument. It was not difficult to produce ample empirical material against his thesis: 'These cases soon became the basis of a large anti-Hermens literature' (Eckstein 1968, 447). In fact Hermens' model 'became almost an object of ridicule among serious scholars' (Mayer 1989, 150).

The latter part of Hermens' implict model, the relationship between party system fragmentation and government stability, received less attention in this early debate. A more detailed presentation of empirical research concerning this relationship will be made in Chapter 3. At this stage it is sufficient to say that the proposed connection between party system fragmentation and political instability at least can not be refuted altogether in the light of existing empirical evidence. Below, therefore, the main arguments concerning this relationship in the orginal theoretical literature will be summarized.

Why should the fragmentation of the party system make a difference? What theoretical arguments were presented in support of the 'myth of multipartism' (Dodd 1976, 10)? Hermens and his followers are much more explicit concerning the effects of the electoral system than on this point. Nevertheless, three groups of arguments can readily be culled from this literature:

1 Multiparty systems do not produce natural governmental *majorities*. Governments are either minority cabinets at the mercy of the parliamentary opposition or they are coalitions. Coalitions are inherently unstable because they, unlike cabinets in two-party systems, lack the clear support of the people as expressed in electoral results. The participating parties will remain wary and suspicious of each other, anxious not to lose electoral support by far-reaching compromises (Hermens 1958, 169, 174). Or as Downs puts it, government coalitions under multipartism are constantly subjected to centripetal as well as centrifugal forces. On the one hand, the necessity to keep the coalition together drives the participating parties toward the center of the ideological spectrum. On the other hand, their desire to win as many votes as possible

may compel them to repeatedly diverge from one another in matters of major principal importance, i.e., to keep a distinct political profile of their own (Downs 1957, 156-159). Thus, governments under multipartism, be they minority cabinets or majority coalitions, tend to be chronically unstable.

2   Multiparty systems lack the *integrative capacity* typical of two-party systems. The latter encourage integration in two ways. Within the parties, there is a 'constant process of adjustment', whereby diverging demands are reconciled with each other before they reach the parliamentary level (Hermens 1958, 166). 'In addition to intra-party integration there is inter-party integration; it results from the need to reconcile the undecided voter who stands between the major parties' (Ibid., 174). Thus the party system in itself functions in a way which tends to discourage those kinds of extreme views that may endanger the stability of the system.

Multiparty systems, by contrast, foster 'isms' based on rigid principles. Quite unlike the flexible tendencies typical of party ideologies in two-party systems, politics in multiparty systems easily becomes a mere reflection of social class conflict. The survival of each party is dependent on the continued vitality of these conflicts. Furthermore, parties with similar views will paradoxically enough 'be likely to attack one another more than parties substantially different from their own' because they compete for the same segment of the electorate. In sum, multipartism encourages segmentation and social conflict and creates political competition even where cooperation and integration would seem to be rational (Hermens 1958, 178-180, 204-205; cf. also Downs 1957, 115).

3 Since the parties in a two-party system tend to be characterized by 'flexible tendencies' rather than by rigid ideologies, 'their alternation in power need not interfere with political continuity...as soon as a party takes over the reins of government it will be practical and pragmatic enough to take over existing institutions and existing policies as they are and try to modify them gradually rather than to tear up everything root and branch' (Hermens 1958, 177-178). Parties that represent narrow class or group interests, by contrast, cannot provide the necessary continuity and stability. They are 'concerned with one particular issue, and the government has to meet a number of related issues at

the same time'. Moreover, as they 'come and go', the electorate will not know 'whom to hold to account if something went wrong' (Ibid., 181).

In sum, the stability characteristic of the two-party system and absent in multiparty systems rested on several sturdy pillars: cabinet cohesion, reduction of social cleavages, policy continuity and political accountability.

Consociationalism

After World War II, the international standing of the Anglo-American world was high, whereas large parts of continental Europe had suffered severe losses of prestige due to both the authoritarian regimes that had taken over in the interwar period and the wartime policies of these regimes. Implicitly or explicitly, much of the early postwar research on democracy and democratization looked upon England and the United States as models of democratic government for the rest of the world. Political sociologists such as Gabriel Almond came to regard social and cultural heterogeneity as threats to democracy, while those researchers who were more interested in institutional and organizational aspects of politics stressed the superiority of two-party systems and majoritarian electoral arrangements over multipartism and proportional representation.

From the 1960s on, this research began to receive increasing criticism from a group of researchers, many of whom were specialists in continental European politics. These scholars pointed to the fact that a number of European countries characterized by social and cultural heterogeneity as well as by political fragmentation displayed long periods of continuous democratic rule. They argued that the crucial factor explaining these cases was not social or institutional structures as such but *elite cooperation*, the behavior of responsible leaders interacting with one another. Where a cooperative attitude prevailed despite social and institutional complexity these scholars pointed to *consociational* mechanisms as the underlying cause. The term consociationalism, as this line of research at large, is usually associated with Arend Lijphart.

Lijphart does not deny that social heterogeneity and political fragmentation are problematic as such from the point of view of democratization or the stability of democratic rule. However, he finds that these factors have been treated in a reductionist manner which tends to overemphasize their explanatory power. His two main books on the subject, *Democracy in Plural Societies* (1977) and *Democracies* (1984) are largely parts of the same research process. However, the first book places a stronger emphasis on social and cultural structures; to a large extend, it can be seen as a reaction against the research tradition associated with Almond. The second book is more oriented toward the political system as such. It starts out with a description of the 'Westminster model', the British model of parliamentary democracy and goes on to analyze the alternative model, now termed Consensus Democracy.

Those who argue for the superiority of two-partism can, according to Lijphart, be criticized on several important points. For one, they were preoccupied with the large democratic countries and 'with the contrast between the stable British and American two-party systems and the unstable multiparty systems of the German Weimar Republic, the French Third and Fourth Republics, and postwar Italy' (1984, 111). This being the case, it was not far-fethced to attribute the instability of the latter regimes to the fragmentation of their party systems. A look at Scandinavia, the Benelux countries and Switzerland offers quite a different view of the relationship between party systems and political stability and calls the simplistic interpretation of the 'myth of multipartism' into question.

Second, Lijphart questions the use of cabinet instability as an indicator of 'fundamental regime instability' (ibid.). He does admit that multiparty systems tend to be characterized by more short-lived cabinets than two-party systems, but this 'instability' may have several functions that do not necessarily place the democratic system as such at risk. The lack of cabinet continuity is frequently balanced by a high degree of personal continuity; what looks like a regime shift often simply entails a reshuffle of the same pool of ministers as in previous cabinets. Moreover, Lijphart emphasizes that these changes frequently reflect a responsiveness at the cabinet level vis-à-vis the will of the parliament. Conversely: *'If cabinet durability is an indicator of anything, it shows the dominance of the cabinet over the legislature...*[t]he majoritarians' confusion of cabinet stability may be partly explained in terms of their preference for powerful and dominant executives' (p. 113, emphasis in original).

Third, Lijphart points to the contradiction present in most *plaidoyers* for two-partism: on the one hand, these authors claim that the parties in a two-party system will be moderate and tend toward the center; on the other hand, the same parties are said to present the electorate with a clear choice between alternative programs. In fact, the literature here merges American moderation with British adversarialism thus creating a two-party world which really does not exist (Ibid.).

Fourth, the claim about one-party responsibility for government actions is again a typical British feature. The American system of checks and balances always permits both parties to exert government power either through the presidency or through Congress. It is not two-partism per se but two-partism in a pure parliamentary system that is characterized by one-party responsibility.

Finally, two-party theory implicitly relies on the assumption that there is one issue-dimension which is clearly more salient than all others, i.e., the left-right cleavage. In most democracies, however, a multi-dimensional issue structure prevails; in such a situation 'a two-party system must be regarded as an electoral strait-jacket that can hardly be regarded as democratically superior to a multiparty system reflecting all the major issue alternatives' (p. 114).

How do we know a consociational system when we see one? Lijphart's description has shifted somewhat over the years, but the basic elements are largely the same in both of his major works. In contrast to majoritarian democracy, consociational practices aim at restraining majority rule. They encourage the *sharing of power* between the majority and the minority; the main instrument is the use of *grand coalitions* instead of one-party cabinets. Also, they work toward a *dispersal of power*: a separation of powers between the executive and the legislature, bicameralism and the existence of several minority parties are typical features. *Proportional representation* guarantees a *'fair distribution of power'*. Furthermore, power is often *delegated* to territorially or nonterritorially organized groups. Finally, in a clear contrast to majoritarianism, consociational systems contain *formal limits on power*: the main instrument is the use of *minority veto* (1984, 21-30, cf. 1977, 25-44).

Consociational practices and arrangements naturally reflect social and cultural conditions in those countries in which they appear. They are means to cope with heterogeneity and complexity within a democratic framework. They are expected to appear in polities characterized by the existence of several population segments of roughly equal size and a balanced power relation among them. A high degree of autonomy within each segment is also conducive to consociationalism. On the other hand, there must be overarching loyalties common to the segments to hold the nation together. Crosscutting rather than cumulative social cleavages make for consociationalism. Finally, the size of the polity also plays a role: consociationalism is expected to be more common in small rather than large systems (1977, 52-103).

In sum, the theory of consociationalism argues that social and political complexity as such is no deadly threat to democracy. Democracy must find institutional and organizational expressions that match the actual conditions in a society. Consociational mechanisms are a way to combine democratic rule with socio-cultural pluralism. From the point of view of stability, consociationalism is a much more pragmatic solution than any attempt to impose a majoritarian 'straitjacket' to a plural society.

The Structure of the Book

This book is not out to prove that one of the above theories is wrong and the other is right or even that one is better than the other. Rather, an agnostic and instrumental view of the theories prevails. It is an empirical task to demonstrate to what expect they explain political stability and the destiny of democracy in interwar Europe; *a priori*, both of them seem quite reasonable and none of them extremely unlikely to find empirical support. It should, moreover, be stressed that they are not mutually exclusive; it is equally probable that they are complementary, i.e., help explain different cases.

The empirical part of the book starts with a brief sketch the the interwar crisis itself. In the same chapter, the cases selected for the systematic analysis are presented in the form of short narratives. The empirical testing of the theories is structured according to the chronology which is present in the theoretical literature. The starting point is the early literature on party system fragmentation. The 'fragmentation thesis' will be tested with the aid of a relatively large number of cases and with an emphasis on quantitative research techniques. After that, the 'challenger', the theory of consociationalism will be subjected to empirical examination. This work involves a number of fairly detailed case studies. The cases will be selected on the basis of the results of the first empirical analysis. The emphasis is on cases which seem to contradict the theory of fragmentation, and the main question is whether consociationalism is the key to those cases which cannot be explained with the aid of fragmentation theory. Since the two main empirical involve somewhat different methods and data, the operational choices will be discussed separately in connection with these two chapters.

Chapter 2

Breakdown and Survival: the Crisis of Democracy in Interwar Europe

The main objective of this chapter is to discuss the criteria for the selection of empirical cases and to give a descriptive account of the political development in interwar Europe in general as well as in each individual country included in the study. The first task requires a discussion of some of the central concepts which were already used in Chapter 1 without any attempts to characterize their essential contents. The second part - the bulk of this chapter - gives a necessary factual background to the systematic analyses of the two theories tested in the book. At the same time, it involves an application of the conceptual discussion so as to permit conclusions about which cases represent 'the survival' and which countries the 'breakdown' of democracy.

Democracy, Crisis and Breakdown

Whatever definition of 'democracy' one wishes to present, one is likely to encounter as much criticism as support on the part of scholars and other readers. The fact that outright opposition to democracy has diminished over time has not brought us any closer to a generally acceptable definition of the concept. Rather, as Giovanni Sartori has pointed out, our age is a paradoxical one of 'confused democracy': 'Up until the 1940s people knew what democracy was and either liked or rejected it; since then we all claim to like democracy but no longer know... what it is' (1987, 6). At the same time, on a more practical level there is an extensive consensus on which the world's democracies are or have been in the past. We know a democracy when we see one, but we seem to fail to catch its essentials in an inclusive definition.

This study adopts a pragmatic approach and does not pretend to have arrived at a fully-fledged definition of the elusive concept of democracy. Naturally, some criteria are necessary for the sorting out of democracies from non-democracies. These criteria form, however, a list of essential features rather than a coherent definition.

Basically, the co-existence of universal political rights and civil liberties is the foundation of a democratic system. The former refers mainly to the right to participate in free and competitive elections, whereas the latter pertains to the freedom of speech and association (Lijphart 1984, 37). 'Free elections' means the freedom to formulate political alternatives, the periodic validation of the political leaders' claim to rule and the absence of fraud and overt violence in the electoral process. Moreover, the democratic process must include all effective political offices. All members of the political community, irrespective of their political orientation, must be allowed to participate in the democratic process (Linz 1978, 5).

Even when a seemingly uncontroversial list of this kind is used to delineate the concept of democracy, one may note a certain shift in the rigor with which it has been applied to different historical periods. 'Today "democracy" implies at least universal male suffrage, but perhaps in the past it would extend to the regimes with property, taxation, occupational, or literacy requirements of an earlier period, which limited suffrage to certain social groups', Linz writes (1978, 5). By the same token, Lijphart (1984, 39) admits that the inclusion of Switzerland, the United States and France among the polities which have been 'continuously democratic since about World War II' is somewhat problematic: female citizens in Switzerland were not given the right to vote until 1971; up until the 1970s, there were restrictions for the voting rights of black Americans; France briefly suspended regular democratic processes in connection with the transition from the Fourth to the Fifth Republic. All this goes to say that the classification of states as democracies at all times will be subject to some inconsistency and even ethnocentrism; it underlines the necessity of clearly demonstrating the grounds of classification in each individual case.

Similarly, 'crisis' is a notoriously ill-defined concept in political science as well as in the general political discourse. In fact, the term is today strongly inflated; there is hardly any problem or difficulty in politics which is not described as a 'crisis' in the political debate and in the media. There is no need in this context to dwell on the extensive and continuous scholarly debate about the concept of crisis (for an overview, see Wiberg 1988, 175-233; cf. also Svensson 1986, 132-135). Instead, the problem is again on a more practical level. The *interwar* crisis in Europe seems to mean different things to different authors largely depending on whether economic or political factors are stressed. To many the interwar crisis is synonymous with the Great Depression, from late 1929 up until the mid-1930s (e.g., Zimmermann 1988) Others distinguish between two separate economically determined crises, one subsequent to the immediate post World War boom and the other of course being the Great Depression (cf. Luebbert 1991, 191-233). Those underlining the political nature of the crisis, however, tend to view the entire interwar period as a continuous crisis of democracy (cf. Linz 1991, 231-280; Tingsten 1933, 3-22, 57-63).

It would naturally be highly misleading to deny or belittle the economic background of the interwar crisis. Especially in the 1930s the breakdown of democracy has clear connections with the worsened economic circumstances of large parts of the population. The fact that the crisis became a *crisis of democracy* was, however, due to the existence of groups and movements that saw the political system as the cause of the problems. These groups were certainly aided by the economic crisis, but they were present and active throughout Europe long before the onset of the Great Depression.

Consequently, the present study sees the interwar period as a whole as a crisis of European democracy. Democracy faced real and active opposition from three different quarters: revolutionary socialism, fascism and traditional monarchism. The two latter were in some cases intertwined. The importance of monarchism was greatest at the beginning of the period, while the fascist challenge reached its peak during the Great Depression. Communism was a real threat to democracy during most of the period, although it lost some of its appeal in the course of the 1930s.

Throughout the 1920s and the 1930s, therefore, democratic institutions were subjected to repeated attacks and challenges from these antidemocratic groups. Already in the 1920s, several newly established democratic regimes went under in the face of these pressures. For those countries where democracy weathered this storm the period entailed serious parliamentary instability and prolonged labor market conflicts. In the course of the 1930s, another group of

European states switched to authoritarian regimes, while several countries experienced entirely new political constellations in an attempt to meet the anti-democratic pressures from the right as well as from the left.

'Breakdown' of democracy evidently implies that the political practices in a country shift from the kinds of instituitions and processes described above to a situation where these characteristics no longer apply. While we agree with Sartori in his assertion that it is important to avoid 'degreeism' especially with view to what systems are democratic and what are not (1991, 248-249) it is clear that there is some variation among democratic as well as non-democratic states. As concerns the former group, the fundamental political freedoms together with political accountability form the basic defining element. To this, however, there is one important exception. Restrictions in the right of explicitly anti-democratic (communist or fascist) movements to organize themselves and contest elections have as such not been regarded as sufficient to cause a state to be defined as 'non-democratic' at a given point in time. Over and above this, there is - as will be evident from the descriptive accounts below - a great deal of variation in the degree to which opposition and human rights were suppressed in the 'non-democratic' group of countries in the interwar period.

Europe between the World Wars

Europe immediately after the World War looked perhaps more democratic than it has ever done in its entire history. In Western and Northern Europe, the years preceding the war had entailed a steady march toward mass democracy. In fact, liberal and radical groups in the Western Entente countries had to a large extent perceived of the war as a struggle between democracy and antiquated monarchical regimes. Through the entrance of the United States into the war and the separate peace between Russia and the central Powers the frontline became quite clear: it was the non-democratic Great Powers of Europe that bore the responsibility for the war (Tingsten 1933, 16). Woodrow Wilson's call to make Europe 'safe for democracy' was far from just an idealistic or altruistic gesture toward a continent ravaged by war. It was a victor's assessment as to what measures should be imposed on the defeated in order to guarantee that they would not threaten the world again.

An unprecedented wave of democratization and constitutional reform washed over Europe right after the end of the war. Those western countries that had not become fully-fledged democracies before 1918 removed the last obstacles to universal suffrage and parliamentarism. Revolutions in the wake of the defeat of the Central Powers paved the way for a transition to democracy in Germany as well as in the Austrian state which followed the collapse of the Austro-Hungarian Empire. In a majority of the new states which emerged from the dissolution of the Habsburg and Russian empires - in Poland, Czechoslovakia, Lithuania, Latvia, Estonia and Finland - unequivocally democratic constitutions and practices were established. In some other countries - Greece, Rumania, Albania, Hungary, Rumania and Bulgaria - the situation remained somewhat more ambiguous. Throughout Europe, however, constitutional reforms and political changes in the direction of democratic rule were the order of the day (Newman 1970, 21-34, 225-227; Linz 1991, 231-239).

Europe may momentarily have looked democratic, but 'safe for democracy' she was not. The 1917 Bolshevik Revolution had already created a massive challenge to what the Soviet regime and its adherents elsewhere renounced as an expression of bourgeois hegemony. In Germany, Austria, Hungary, Estonia and Finland the Russian Revolution inspired attempts at a revolutionary takeover on the part of large segments of the working class movement in 1918-19; elsewhere, strikes and other manifestations gave expression to increasing maximalist tendencies in the labor movement. Economic hardships and structural transformations in the wake of the war fomented these tendencies. Large groups of war veterans found it difficult to adjust to a society which had rapidly left time-honored agrarian forms of economic and social life behind and replaced them with an industrial economy in anonymous big cities.

On the right, the revolutionary challenge was largely blamed on democracy; it was parliamentarism that allowed treacherous marxism to organize itself and seek representation in the political system. In the defeated countries revanchism aggravated these tendencies. The privileged groups of the prewar autocracies regarded democracy as part and parcel of the unjust postwar settlement which had deprived their country of its rightful place among the nations and of considerable part of its territory. Elsewhere, in Italy in particular, victory in the war had not satisfied the territorial claims nationalist groups had made (Linz 1980, 153-189).

From the very beginning, therefore, European democracy faced considerable difficulties. In some countries, it never really left its cradle. Elsewhere, emergency powers were momentarily introduced in the face of political and economic chaos; this was not only the case in Germany and Austria but also in such relatively established democracies as Belgium and France (Tingsten 1933, 18). Italy became the first 'old' democracy to succumb to authoritarian pressures subsequent to Mussolini's March on Rome in 1922. The following year, subsequent to a military rebellion, Spanish parliamentarism was abolished; it was to re-emerge for a five-year period in 1931. In 1926 Portugal and Poland switched to authoritarian governments; the same year, a military revolt put an end to democracy in Lithuania. The Great Depression hit a continent where the crisis of democracy had already reaped a sad harvest.

This is hardly the place for an extensive account of the economic development that followed the crash at the New York Stock Exchange in October, 1929 (for detailed accounts, see Garraty 1986; Gourevitch, 1986; Zimmermann and Saalfeld, 1988; Eichengreen and Hatton 1988). Suffice it to say that the capitalist world economy suffered its most dramatic slump ever. Within a matter of a couple of years, unemployment passed the twenty or even thirty per cent mark in most countries. Industrial production fell dramatically, being in many cases merely half of the highest figure reached after the war. Farm income displayed a similar course, and farm foreclosures *en masse* became the order of the day. For most countries, the depression culminated in 1932 or 1933. Since the various countries differed widely as to their economic structure - the level of industrialization, in particular - the 'physical appearance' of the crisis was different from country to country. Moreover, for some of the states of Eastern and Southern Europe it is difficult to obtain reliable data describing the effects of the depression. Nevertheless, it seems reasonable to argue that the depression was a universal phenomenon which affected all European nations in a roughly similar manner. A comparison between highly industrialized Belgium and predominantly rural Finland, for instance, would clearly seem to support such a conclusion (cf. De Meur and Berg-Schlosser 1990; Karvonen 1989). For all of Europe, politics in the first half of the 1930s were indeed, as Gourevitch has put it, 'politics in hard times' (1986).

The political response is well-known from the previous literature. The support of fascist and right wing authroritarian movements peaked everywhere in Europe in the 1930s, in most cases during the depression or in its immediate aftermath (Merkl 1980, 756). In 1933, Hitler's *Machtergreifung* in Germany marked the beginning of a new series of authoritarian takeovers. In 1933-34, parliamentary democracy was abolished in Estonia, Latvia and Austria. In 1936, the outbreak of the Spanish Civil War marked the end of the short-lived Second Republic. In several other countries democracy seemed to be on the verge of its demise as acute threats of fascist takeovers emerged. In Finland in 1932, in France in 1934 as well as in Belgium in 1934-36, these threats were averted through resolute government action and through new forms of political consensus among democratic parties and organizations. Irrespective of the outcome, the 1930s witnessed the culmination of political violence and overt fascist action throughout Europe.

By 1937, the political map of Europe therefore looked radically different from the one in 1920. The *majority* of the European states were non-democracies. Central, Southern and Eastern Europe were almost entirely nondemocratic, whereas democracy retained its positions in Western and Northern Europe (see map).

National trajectories

The character of this research requires that both countries where democracy went under and states where it survived the interwar crisis be included in the empirical analysis. Sixteen countries form the units of analysis in this study. All eleven states where democracy survived are included, whereas the cases of 'breakdown' number five. This somewhat asymmetrical sample is the result of a combination of practical and analytical circumstances. For many of the 'non-democracies', reliable data of the kind necessary for the systematical analysis are extremely difficult to come by. At the same time many of them have so short and unstable periods of democracy in their pre- and postwar history that the analysis of the breakdown of democracy is rendered quite uncertain.

Below, descriptive accounts of the highlights of the interwar political developments are presented for each of the countries separately. The five cases of 'breakdown' are presented first in a chronological order, beginning with Italy, the earliest case of transition from democracy to authoritarianism.

Italy

Italy is in many ways a special case among European states in the 19th and early 20th century. It combines early and gradual democratization - typical of the stable democracies of Western Europe - with an early breakdown of democracy after the World War. The Italian path to democracy is in itself rather curious. In terms of concrete measures in the direction of fully democratic practices the country made steady progress. At the same time, the 1848 Piedmontese constitution adopted by the unified Italian state in 1861 was never subject to a throrough revision despite these significant changes. In 1882, the number of enfranchised citizens quadrupled as a result of an extension of suffrage, comprising nearly thirty per cent of the male population. In 1912 suffrage was extended to all men above the age of 30; the following year, universal manhood suffrage was introduced.

Meanwhile, the country was operating under a constitution which prescribed monarchical executive rule. There was no codified principle of parliamentarism in the constitution, and the division of labor between the executive and the legislature was somewhat ambiguous, there being no clear stipulations about the areas that were to be regulated through laws and others where executive decrees were to apply. Nevertheless, parliamentary accountability was in practice introduced early. The monarch utilized his right to dissolve the Lower House of the parliament, the Chamber of Deputies, rather frequently, but this was done at the initiative of the cabinet, which excercised the powers granted to the monarch by the Constitution. The cabinet itself normally resigned due to a vote of non-confidence or a comparable measure on the part of the parliamentary majority.

In terms of the party system, the Italian development resembled that in many contemporary Western European countries. The original 'French' pattern with loosely defined 'Left' and 'Right' gradually crumbled. In 1895, the Socialist Party entered the parliament; it was soon beset with internal strife between various factions, which, i.a., led to the exit of the syndicalists in 1906 (Fritsche 1987, 45-59; Allum 1973, 3-7).

Italian politics remained largely personalistic and clientelistic during the prewar years. It was the various notables leading the parliamentary groups rather than the party cleavages that mattered. Frequent cabinet resignations occurred, but the same pool of ministers tended to return to the government after each reshuffle; elections did not produce alternative cabinet constellations. Moreover, a typical Italian feature was that foreign policy questions rather than domestic issues produced the most profound disagreements. It was in such a disagreement over the Italian role in the world war that the origins of the eventual fascist takeover largely lay (Tingsten 1930, 9-30).

In contradistinction to most other belligerent nations, the Italians remained divided over the country's participation in the war. The non-interventionist majority in the parliament succeeded in keeping the country outside the war until May, 1915. The predominantly 'pacifist' Socialist Party split up, as the interventionist wing led by Benito Mussolini left the party. Nationalist groups saw the treaty of Versailles as a treachery against Italy depriving it of the Adriatic terrotories (including the city of Trieste) they regarded as the rightful property of victorious Italy; 'Italy won the war but lost the peace'. Together with the increasing radicalization of the socialist movement, this added to the polarization of Italian politics (Baglieri 1980, 321-323; Jungar 1991, 250-251).

A new electoral law adopted in 1918 prescribed proportional representation. It was first applied in 1919 and paved the way for increased fractionalization in the party system. A newly established Catholic Party and the socialists emerged victorious, gathering 100 and 156 of the 508 seats, respectively. Various liberal groups gained a total of 230 seats and numerous small parties the remainder. The socialists were thus the largest single party; this led many socialists to believe that the party could gain political power on its own. Those socialists who argued for cooperation with democratic liberal groups in the face of the mounting threat from Mussolini's fascists and other extreme nationalists were hindered by a fear of an internal split between reformists and revolutionaries in the PSI. With the growing strength of the socialist vote and a rapidly increasing party membership the revolutionaries gained confidence and switched to direct action manifested primarily through the famous factory occupations of 1920. This finally brought about a split in the PSI, as the Italian Communist Party was founded in January, 1921. During most of 1921, the country was in practice in a state of civil war between revolutionary socialists and fascists. Having crushed a General Strike intended as an anti-fascist manifestation Mussolini directed his black-shirted columns toward the capital in the famous March on Rome in October, 1922. As a result Luigi Facta's cabinet resigned and turned over the cabinet power to Mussolini (Hermens 1958, 391-396).

For all practical purposes, the March on Rome signified the breakdown of Italian democracy. Nevertheless, Mussolini first embarked on a relatively moderate and cooperative cabinet line. His coalition included several liberal ministers, and the socialists were allowed to continue in parliament. In 1923, however, a rather peculiar electoral law was introduced guaranteeing the fascist-dominated National Alliance nearly two-thirds of the parliamentary seats. The final showdown took place in 1924, when Giacomo Matteotti headed the socialist front against Mussolini. After having ajourned the parliament several times and after Matteotti had been assassinated, Mussolini finally proclaimed the fascist dictatorship on January 3, 1925.

Germany

In contrast to Italy, Germany experienced a fundamental constitutional change in the aftermath of the World War. The monarchical form of government of Wilhelminian Germany was replaced by the Weimar Constitution of 1919, largely a product of a coalition of social democrats, liberal democrats and the Catholic Center Party. The social democrats were the dominant force in this coalition. The opposition against the constitution consisted of the nationalist wing, which argued for a continued monarchical rule. The German People's Party was the more moderate element of this opposition, and it was soon willing to strike deals with the republican parties and groups, whereas the

German National Party continued its ardent resistance against the Weimar Constitution (Nicholls 1985, 20-37, 50-62; Koch 1984, 259-266).

The Weimar Constitution was strictly democratic, but it contained a dualistic element which separated it from the parliamentary democracies of Northwestern Europe. On the one hand, it prescribed parliamentarism; the government was to depend on the will of the majority in the *Reichstag*. On the other hand, it provided for a strong, popularly elected President. Among other things, the President could dissolve the parliament and call for new elections. Moreover, he was invested with emergency powers which enabled him to suspend some of the constitutional provisions in critical situations (Koch 1984, 266-271; Hermens 1958, 329-339).

The parliamentary majority of the original Weimar coalition was lost in the 1920 election. Instead, the German People's Party entered the government; this was a clear sign that the industrial and finance communities no longer wished to boycott the republican state. As for the more extreme nationalists, they had far from reconciled themselves to the republic. In particular, they criticized the political leadership for acquiesence vis-à-vis foreign powers. The war reparations Germany was obliged to pay were claimed to be unreasonable. The French occupation of the Ruhr in 1923 made the foreign policy crisis acute. At the same time, an economic crisis and the rise to regional power of radical socialists in Saxony and Thuringia signalled more general turbulence in German politics. In conservative Bavaria, the national socialists gained momentum and made their first more notable appearance in connection with the abortive Beer Hall Putsch. The acute crisis was met through the creation of the hitherto broadest government coalition comprising the People's Party, the social democrats and all parties between them on the left-right scale (Pachter 1978, 116).

The nationalistic wave was strong, however, and in the May 1924 elections both the German National Party and the national socialists made considerable gains; the Nazis entered the *Reichstag* with 32 seats out of a total of 479. Cabinet politics came to be conservative-dominated for several years to come, and the social democrats were to remain in opposition until 1928. All the same, this was a period of relative stability. Especially in the field of foreign policy, important settlements were reached during this period. The Dawes Plan (to be followed by the Young Plan in 1929), the Treaty of Locarno and

German membership in the League of Nations stand as important landmarks of progress during this period. As to the economy, the period was characterized by increased productivity and a rising standard of living (Nicholls 1985, 83-104; Pachter 1978, 101-136).

In 1928, the tables were turned as the social democrats made their greatest electoral gains ever while both the National Party and the national socialists lost considerably. A coalition under the leadership of Hermann Müller took office. The National Party and the nazis drifted closer to one another as a result. In the fall of 1929, they jointly demanded a referendum aimed at a revision of Germany's treaties on war reparations as well as of parts of the Treaty of Versailles. The referendum, which was largely perceived as a vote for or against the Weimar Republic, was a bitter disappointment to the nationalists: merely some fifteen per cent of the voters supported the proposal (Conze 1964, 222-224).

If the Republic had won in the political sphere, the economic horizon looked far worse. Already before the Great Depression hit Germany the economic situation had deteriorated; with the depression it soon became untenable. Müller's cabinet resigned in March, 1930, due to a disagreement over the budget. It was followed by Heinrich Brüning's cabinet supported only by the centrist parties. As this cabinet failed to mobilize a majority behind its budget proposal, it proceeded to prepare for the dissolution of the *Reichstag*, which took place in July, 1930.

From this time on, the parliamentary mechanism no longer functioned in Germany. The *Reichstag* assembled only sporadically. The national socialists leaped from twelve seats in 1928 to 107 in the 1930 election; the centrist parties in particular lost votes to the NSDAP. The austerity measures introduced by the government were insufficient to solve the economic problems while at the same time provoking a great deal of protest from the citizenry. The storm troops of the Nazis increasingly took to the streets to terrorize their political opponents and Jews (Kühnl 1985, 207-221; Tingsten 1936, 23-25).

The last attempt of the original Weimar coalition to save the republic was their united support for Hindenburg who ran against Hitler in the 1932 presidential election. The attempt was in itself successful as Hindenburg won the second ballot. In terms of a political outcome, however, something quite different ensued. Hindenburg suddenly dismissed the Brüning cabinet in May, 1932; a month before, Brüning had issued a ban against the Nazi storm troops. A conspicuously conservative cabinet under Franz von Papen took office and proceeded to relegalize the SA and the SS (Pachter 1978, 191-198; Nicholls 1985, 105-123).

The elections held in July 1932 gave the NSDAP its greatest victory ever: with some 37 per cent of the vote and 230 seats it was by far the largest party in the country. A conflict between Hitler and von Papen over the position as Chancellor ensued. Another dissolution of the *Reichstag* followed. A new election in November gave the Nazis a loss of 34 seats, whereas the Communist Party won its greatest victory ever mustering 100 seats. This parliament was, however, never to assemble. The center of gravity in German politics shifted to secret negotiations between Hindenburg, Hitler, von Papen and Alfred Hugenberg, the National Party leader. As a result of these negotiations, Hitler took office as Chancellor on January 30, 1933 (Craig 1978, 560-568).

What followed was a transition to dictatorship which was more rapid and more throrough than in the case of Italy. The communists were excluded from the *Reichstag*; on the 23 of March only only the social democrats voted against a law which in practice granted Hitler unlimited authority.

Austria

The collapse of Austrian democracy is frequently seen as part and parcel of the German development. Hitler was, after all, an Austrian, and as of the *Anschluss* of 1938 Austria's political course was identical with that of the Third Reich. Democracy had, however, collapsed several years earlier, and the principal actors in that development were of unmistakably indigenous Austrian variety.

After the collapse of the Habsburg empire the predominantly German-speaking provinces proclaimed the Republic of Austria in 1918. The constitution adopted in October, 1920 was distinctly democratic and parliamentary. It provided for a bicameral legislature, with the popularly elected National Council (*Nationalrat*) as the center of power; all men and women over the age of twenty had the right to participate in the elections. The Federal Council (*Bundesrat*) was chosen by the provincial parliaments and had fairly limited powers. Moreover, the President was to be mainly a representative figure lacking both veto rights and the power to dissolve the parliament (Gulick 1948, 95-111; Andics 1984, 74-76).

As a society, Austria was divided into three distinct segments (*Lager*) that led largely separate existencies and remained more or less hostile toward each other. A strong pan-German opinion demanded that Austria be joined with Germany; its main representative in politics was the Greater German People's Party. The social democrats, who were radical 'Austro-Marxists' and tended to regard the republic as a provisional stage rather than an end in itself, controlled the mass of workers in the cities, especially in 'Red Vienna'. An equally strong force was, however, the catholic movement headed by the Christian Social Party. This movement retained much of its monarchistic outlook and was oriented toward the catholic world rather than toward Germany; it therefore regarded both the socialists and the *Grossdeutschen* as its opponents (Botz 1980, 192-199).

The paradox of Austrian politics was that the distinctly democratic form of government had no proponents who saw it as their *primary* task to defend democracy; Austria was *'eine Republik ohne Republikaner'* (Hoor 1966, 90-91; Andics 1984, 24-38)). Instead, they concentrated their energies to fighting each other. The position of democracy was rendered even more precarious by the existence of two outright fascist movements. *Heimwehr* was a paramilitary organization within the catholic camp. It demanded the restoration of the monarchy and dreamed ultimately of a catholic *Mitteleuropa* from Rome to Budapest as a sort of a reincarnation of the Habsburg empire. It attacked socialists, Jews as well as the republican form of government. It appeared in elections under the name *Heimatblock*. At the same time, it gained increasing influence within the Christian Social Party. Gradually, a distinctly Nazi movement also emerged. It represented the most extreme German orientation in Austria and was bitterly opposed to *Heimwehr* as well as to both the social democrats and Christian Socials; within the Greater German People's Party it enjoyed considerable support (Kitchen 1980, 52-72; Pauley 1980, 226- 235).

Due to these pressures the constitution was reformed in 1929 giving the President considerably expanded powers. For one, he was to be elected through a direct popular vote. Moreover, he was granted the right to appoint the members of the cabinet as well as to dissolve the parliament (Hoor 1966, 102). In the 1930 elections, the Christian Social Party lost six of its formerly 72 seats. At the same time, *Heimatblock* gained representation winning eight seats in parliament. Moreover, the Land League, a conservative peasant party formed a few years earlier increased its representation to nine seats. The Greater Germans held ten seats at this time. As coalitons including social democrats and nonsocialists were not practised and as the bourgeois camp was internally divided, cabinet formation became difficult. The onset of the Great Depression made matters worse. On top of this, the national socialists inspired by the electoral victories of German nazism now emerged as a factor to be reckoned with.

It was a cabinet led by the Christian Social leader Engelbert Dollfuss that was to form the transition to dictatorship in Austria. Formed in May, 1932, this cabinet originally rested on a parliamentary majority of one vote, supported as it was by the Christians, *Heimatblock* and the Land League. With *Machtergreifung* in Germany the Nazi threat in Austria became increasingly present. In the spring of 1933, Dollfuss therefore decided to make use of a wartime emergency law to issue a ban against the national socialists as well as the communists. As the Constitutional Court was deprived of its right to examine the legality of this measure, this move represented the first definitive step toward authoritarianism. In May the same year Dollfuss decided to assemble the coalition behind the government in the Fatherland Front. The Land League withdrew from the coalition; *Heimwehr* influence in the Fatherland Front increased to a decisive degree. Open and violent clashes between social democratic activists and *Heimwehr* troops took place. The government declared the social democratic organizations illegal in February, 1934. In July the national socialists attempted a coup in connection with which Dollfuss was assassinated. Kurt von Schuschnigg became his successor (Hoor 1966, 103-118; Rath and Schum 1980, 249-253).

When Schuschnigg resumed office Austria was already a dictatorship. In the four years before *Anschluss* a bureaucratic-corporatist state was created. Elections were never held after 1930, and political rights and freedoms were severely restricted.

Estonia

Estonia, which had been part of the Russian empire since 1710, reached independence in 1918. Its secession from Russia was, however, followed by a war in which Estonian nationalist troops fought against both Russian bolsheviks and indigenous revolutionary socialists. The constitution of independent Estonia was proclaimed in June, 1920.

The form of government created through the 1920 constitution was characterized by the dominant position of the parliament. The parliament chose the prime minister, who besides being the chairman of the cabinet fulfilled the representative functions of a formal head of state. Cabinet formation was largely controlled by the parliament in other respects as well. The parliament itself was chosen through free elections based on universal suffrage for men as well as for women. The electoral system was extremely proportional, with the entire country forming one single electoral district. Moreover, the constitution provided for quite a strong element of direct democracy, as referendums ultimately leading to the dissolution of the parliament were possible to arrange (Mägi 1967, 135-172).

Estonian political life was characterized by a highly complex party structure and recurrent executive crises. A great number of small parties were represented in the parliament, and none of the larger parties ever came close to being able to form a majority cabinet on its own (Vardys 1978, 66-67; Mägi 1967, 321-324) At the same time, the extreme left and right wings displayed a growing militancy. In 1924, an abortive communist coup occurred. This fomented the fascist tendencies among the Veterans of the War of Independence. In 1930, these military units were organized as a political movement. The Veterans demanded that political parties be abolished, that marxists and Jews be persecuted relentlessly, that the entire territory of Estonia be colonized by genuine Estonians and that the workers be integrated into the 'national front' (Nolte 1968, 231; Parming 1975, 39-46).

A thorough revision of the constitution had been debated on several occasions earlier. In 1933, the Veterans' demands for a revision gave result. The new constitution was put to a referendum in October, and it received the clear majority of 72 per cent of the voters. The new constitution entailed a radically strengthened executive power. A new presidential office, the Eldest of the State, was granted far-reaching powers over the parliament and the cabinet. He could dissolve the parliament, and new elections did not need to be called until six months later. He had, moreover, the power to appoint and dismiss the cabinet. His right to veto legislation passed by the parliament was next to unlimited. In short, from being an extremely parliament-centered system Estonian politics had shifted to a situation were the affairs of the state could be carried out largely without the participation of the parliament (Vardys 1978, 72-74; Mägi 1967, 270-272).

Having been successful in its 1932-33 referendum campaign, the veterans now turned their attention to the post of the Eldest of the State itself. Impending rumors of a fascist coup led prime minister Jaan Tönisson to declare a state of emergency and to order the closing of the Veterans' organizations. This did not stop the movement from proclaiming General Andres Larka as its candidate to the Presidency. In this situation, the Farmers' Party leader Konstantin Päts carried out a coup on March 12, 1934. The veterans' movement was declared illegal and its leader was arrested. The following year, political parties were dissolved and replaced by a 'Patriotic Front'. A fascist coup was defeated in December, 1935. This was the final blow against Estonian fascism and it consolidated Päts' position considerably. Through a referendum in 1936, the authoritarian form of government was given popular sanction (Rauch 1967, 145-148).

Latvia

The Latvian case is strikingly similar to the course of events in Estonia. Independence from Russia was followed by a civil war and by foreign intervention. In April 1920, peace having been restored a few months earlier, a provisional constituent assembly was elected. Under its auspices a constitution was drafted. It was adopted in 1922.

The 1922 constitution established a parliamentary form of government. The unicameral legislature was composed of 100 deputies, who were elected for a three-year term through equal, secret and direct elections, where all citizens over the age of 21 had the right to participate. As for the relations between cabinet and parliament, the normal parliamentary rule of confidence applied.

The strong position of the legislature was also underlined by the fact that the head of state, the president, was elected by the parliament rather than by popular vote. The president did have certain powers vis-à-vis the parliament; the fact that his veto was a suspensive one for a two-month period and that his right to dissolve the legislature was dependent on the will of the people in a subsequent plebiscite nevertheless underlined his subordinate position (Barr Carson 1956, 300-304).

In ethnic and social terms, Latvia was a fragmented society with large minorities of Germans, Russians and Jews (Svabe 1961, 106; Garleff 1978, 81-85). As the electoral system was highly proportional and since it was extremely easy to nominate candidates for elections, the result was that a great number of parties contested elections. In the four parliaments which held office in independent Latvia between the world wars, a total of forty different parties were represented at one time or another. The two largest parties, the social democrats and the Peasant League had some twenty and fifteen per cent of the seats, respectively. The chairman of the latter party, Karlis Ulmanis, headed seven of the sixteen cabinets that paraded across the political stage between 1920 and 1934 (Bilmanis 1934, 79-81). He and his party made frequent attempts to revise the electoral system by decreasing its proportionality. Each time, however, they met with resistance from the social democrats and the smaller parties who feared that such a reform would give the Peasant League undue influence.

The immediate events preceding the transition to authoritarianism bore also a great deal of resemblance to the course of events in Estonia. Although evidently numerically weaker than their Estonian brethren, the Latvian fascists - the *Perkonkrusts* - stepped up their antidemocratic and antisemitic activity after the onset of the Great Depression. At the same time, Ulmanis failed to reach a consensus with the social democrats regarding appropriate countermeasures against the mounting radicalization of the political spectrum. On the 15th of May, 1934, Ulmanis proclaimed a state of emergency, which in practice amounted to a bloodless coup d'etat. The parliament was dissolved and the cabinet assumed its legislative functions. Political parties were suppressed. In formal terms, the coup was a fact when the president, Alberts Kviesis, failed to call for a national plebiscite which was required by the constitution if the parliament was to be dissolved (Svabe 1961, 106-109).

The Ulmanis regime never became quite as totalitarian than some of the outright fascist governments elsewhere in Europe. In comparison with Estonia, however, it perhaps moved closer to the fascist pattern of government. The corporate order of state introduced gradually from 1935 onwards bore clear signs of influence from fascist states further south on the European continent.

England

English democracy is a result of several centuries of gradual and steady development under strictly constitutional forms. The balance of power inherent in the constitutional monarchy passed into parliamentarism in the course of the 19th Century. A series of reform acts paved the way for extended democracy: 1832, 1867, 1872, 1884, 1911, 1918 and 1928 represent steps on the way from franchise for two per cent of the population to universal suffrage for men as well as for women. The 1911 House of Lords Reform is particularly notable from a constitutional point of view. It left the upper house of the parliament with merely a limited suspensive veto right, thus signifying that the House of Commons was the center of political power in England (Bentley 1985).

Similarly, a high degree of continuity over the centuries is characteristic of the British party system. An alternation in power between the liberals and the conservatives, which can be seen as the heirs of the whigs and tories, respectively, was typical of British politics throughout the 19th Century and up until the First World War. The wartime coalition between liberals and conservatives under the leadership of David Lloyd George finally produced the most important change in the history of the 20th Century British party system. The demise of this coalition was followed by the rise to prominence of the Labor Party in the 1922 elections, while the liberals suffered an electoral loss from which they never recovered (Pugh 1985, 223-240).

British politics in the late 19th and early 20th Century was at least as preoccupied with the satus of the Empire than with the question of domestic democratization. If anything, the Irish question could have endangered the stability of English politics to a decisive degree. From 1880s on, a series of abortive attempts were made to push the Irish Home Rule Bill through the Houses. Meanwhile, the growing impatience of the Irish population produced acts of terror culminating in a de facto state of war between the Irish Republican Army and British troops. The proclamation of the Irish Free State in 1922 was accompanied by a civil war which lasted until 1923. Nevertheless, it proved to be a satisfactory solution to the Irish problem.

English politics in the 1920s was marked by the growing importance of socio-economic conflicts and the concomitant growth of the Labour Party. The conservatives worked for protectionism within the framework of the empire, while the liberals favored free trade. Labour harbored far-reaching nationalization schemes and demanded a special tax on capital. When Stanley Baldwin's conservative cabinet failed in 1923 to win the majority of the electorate for its proposal for a protective duty system, Ramsay Macdonald formed the first Labour government, which was dependent on the support of the liberals for a majority in Parliament. This cabinet lasted less than a year and was plagued by strikes and a scandal in which Soviet infiltration of English politics through the British Communist Party was implicated. Baldwin assumed office again for almost a five-year period, during which repeated and heated conflicts in the labor market were the order of the day (Taylor 1966, 209-226).

Growing unemployment brought Macdonald and the Labour Party back to power in June, 1929. Again, however, Labour was dependent on liberal support in Parliament. The cabinet's economic reform plans were crushed by the Great Depression. Unemployment approached three million, the international standing of the Pound as well as the confidence in the Gold Standard diminished dramatically. At the same time, Macdonald met increasing resistance within the labor movement. Large groups in the Labour Party demanded an offensive socialist posture. Sir Oswald Mosley, member of the Macdonald government outside the cabinet, demanded radical measures to curb unemployment. When these were not taken he resigned; he would later emerge as the leader of the British Union of Fascists. Meanwhile, the trade unions resisted the cabinet's attempts to cut public spending by limiting unemployment benefits.

In the course of these events, Baldwin finally came to accept the idea of a coalition with Macdonald. The coaliton, which came to be known as the *National Government*, assembled under Macdonald's leadership in August, 1931. It could rely on the majority of the conservative and liberal MPs, but only on a small minority of the labourites. It proceeded to take decisive measures in the field of economic policy. The Gold Standard was abandoned in September, 1931, and the pound was devalued. Foreign trade started to pick up, and cutbacks in government spending and extra taxes balanced the budget. The Treaty of Ottawa stimulated the economic exchange within the commonwealth. In 1935, Baldwin followed Macdonald as Prime Minister in a similar coalition cabinet. When Neville Chamberlain's conservative-liberal cabinet marked the end of the National Government in 1937, the internal political and economic problems that had threatened Britain had largely been overcome and the attention began to focus more and more on the mounting threat against peace in Europe (Pugh 1985, 264-293).

Ireland

From 1801, when the United Kingdom of Great Britain and Ireland was created, until 1922 Ireland was represented in the British Parliament. With the establishment of the Irish Free State, 26 of the altogether 32 Irish counties shifted their parliamentary representation from Westminster to the Free State Parliament in Dublin.

The 1922 Constitution (reformed in 1928 and in 1937) of the Irish Free State created a bicameral legislature. The cabinet leader ('President of the Executive Council') was chosen by the lower house, the *Dáil*; the upper house, the Senate, had a suspensive veto vis-à-vis the lower house. A highly proportional, candidate-centered voting system known as the Single Transferable Vote (STV) was confirmed as the electoral system of the country. The principle of parliamentarism was codified in the constitution. The 1937 constitution abolished the office of the Governor General, the representative of the British monarch. Instead, and Irish President was to be the head of state. The creation of this office did not, however, signify a transfer of power from parliament to executive; the Irish president was primarily a representative figure (Mackie and Rose 1991, 224-227).

From the very beginning, the overshadowing conflict in Irish politics was the status of the Free Republic and its relations to England. The pro-treaty candidates won the first post-civil war election in 1923 with a narrow margin. Their leader William Cosgrave was prime minister until 1932. The opposition led by Eamonn de Valera insisted on total sovereignty from England. In the course of the 1920s, *Fianna Fáil*, the party representing the independence line, gained ground at the expense of *Cumann na nGaedheal* that represented a more conciliatory posture vis-à-vis London. In the 1932 election Fianna Fáil finally became the largest party in the Dáil, controlling 72 of the 153 seats. De Valera formed the new cabinet and proceeded to carry out a total separation from England. The oath to the throne was abolished and the office of the Governor General replaced by an Irish President. The land-annuities due to England under the treaty of 1922 were also withheld. London responded by introducing import duties on Irish goods. It also rejected Irish claims on the six counties in Northern Ireland. The Anglo-Irish relations remained ambiguous and tense throughout the interwar period, and Ireland was a non-belligerent country during the Second World War (Prager 1986, 95 ff.)

Irish politics, in a word, was a sort of single-issue politics based on the relationship with England and what went along with it: the question of independence, the memory of the civil war and the status of Northern Ireland. Basically everything in Irish political life was conditioned by this division. The party system centered around 'republican' and 'unionist' poles. In fact, there was a clear development in the direction of a two-party system during the period. The Labour Party which held 22 seats in the Dáil in 1927 was down to 9 in 1938; the Farmers' Party (15 seats in 1923) had disappeared altogether. For the same reason, 'normal' anti-democratic opposition remained limited in Ireland. The communists managed to gain one seat in 1927, but this was a unique event. The fascist *Blueshirts* attracted a great deal of attention but they failed to mobilize any noteworthy support among the people (Rumpf 1959, 93-176; Manning 1970).

France

The starting point of the French road to fully-fledged democracy dates back to the late 18th century; the 1791 constitution granted the right to vote to all male citizens over 25 years of age who payed a minimum tax. Since then democratization suffered several setbacks. Despite these, one may speak of a fairly steady process of democratization characterized by numerous changes in the constitution and in electoral laws.

The establishment of the Third Republic subsequent to the defeat in the Franco-Prussian war in 1871 signified the definite demise of monarchical rule in France. The constitutional laws adopted in 1875 formed the framework of French politics up until the Second World War. They provided for a bicameral National Assembly. The Chamber of Deputies was elected directly by universal male suffrage, whereas an indirect procedure was used to elect the members of the Senate. The two houses of the Assembly were formally of equal status; in practice the role of the Chamber of Deputies came to be more pronounced. As for the electoral system itself, some instability can be noted. Basically, the two-ballot system with single-member constituencies inherited from the Second Republic was used throughout the period. In 1885, 1919 and 1924, however, varying degrees of proportionality were temporarily introduced into the electoral system. As for the relationship between the executive and the legislature, there was a certain, albeit in practice weak, element of presidentialism in the primarily parliamentary system created by the 1875 constitution. The President of the Republic elected by the National Assembly for a seven-year term was the one who appointed the cabinet ministers. However, these were answerable to the National Assembly both collectively and as individual ministers. In practice the role of the prime minister both in the selection of ministers and in leading the cabinet came to overshadow that of the president (Cole and Campbell 1989, 47-71).

The French party system emerged relatively late considering the early start of democratization in the country. Through most of the 19th Century, a rough left-right division prevailed in the National Assembly. Political parties in the modern sense started to appear around the turn of the century. The establishment of a unified socialist party (the SFIO) in 1905 was particularly significant. The party system remained, however, somewhat elusive throughout the interwar period. There were up to a dozen parties represented in the Chamber of Deputies. Several of them displayed highly varying popular support; at the same time, the boundaries between some of the parties were not at all times clear. The most distinct and numerically strongest group were the left-wing parties, the SFIO and the Radical Republicans/Radical Socialists.

These fractions were of about equal size, and together they commanded about 250 of the approximately 600 seats in the Chamber of Deputies. The centrist block was roughly half this size and divided into twice as many parties with the Left Republicans normally being the largest fraction. On the right, the Republican Union was clearly dominant, although its electoral support and organizational boundaries varied. At most, it mustered over 200 seats in the Chamber (Mackie and Rose 1991, 143-147).

By the same token, cabinet politics was a complex matter in interwar France. No *tendance* had a sufficient parliamentary majority to form a cabinet of a clear rightist, centrist or leftist type. The right and left wings came closest to this, but both types of governments were dependent on at least some support from the political center. Thus, parties of widely varying interests and programs temporarily rallied behind a cabinet; these alliances were inherently unstable, and so was French cabinet politics in general (Dogan 1989, 243-246). This pattern was broken a few times during the period, and the reason was always special circumstances that demanded extraordinary political measures (Greene 1970, 32-48).

During several years after the world war, French politics was preoccupied with foreign policy questions, particularly with the relations to Germany. The war reparations Germany was obliged to pay to France gave rise to a series of crises in the relations between the two countries. When the demilitarized zone in the Ruhr was invaded by German troops as a consequence of communist-led upheavals, France responded by occupying the cities of Frankfurt and Darmstadt in 1920. The question of German war reparations gave rise to a series of cabinet crises in France. The occupation of Düsseldorf, Duisburg and Ruhrort (1921) and a series of international conferences failed to create an overall solution to the problem. The French occupation of the entire Ruhr represented the culmination of the crisis, which finally found a more comprehensive solution in the 1924 Dawes plan (McMillan 1985, 94-97).

Meanwhile, the Ruhr affair triggered off a serious currency crisis. The austerity measures introduced by Raymond Poincaré's cabinet proved unpopular and brought about the first left wing alliance. This failed, however, to present a coherent cabinet alternative. Instead, the deterioration of the currency crisis was followed by the first 'Cabinet of National Unity' headed by Poincaré with the participation and support of all major fractions to the right of the socialists. It managed to overcome the currency crisis and expand France's gold reserves. The late 1920s entailed a period of lessened tensions in the foreign relations field.

The outbreak of Great Depression entailed, just as in the mid-1920s, a rise of the left and the radical centrists. In 1932, Édouard Herriot formed a radical majority cabinet with the support of the socialists. As the general economic crisis was combined with renewed problems related to war reparations from Germany and French war debts to the USA, Herriot did not manage to bring about stability in French politics and his government fell after some months.

Meanwhile, right-wing extremism was gaining momentum and in early 1934 the country seemed on the verge of a violent takeover (Dobry 1989, 511-533). The anti-parliamentary and paramilitary Leagues of right wing extremists attempted a coup by storming the Chamber of Deputies in February. The coup proved abortive and was followed by the second 'Cabinet of National Unity' led by Gaston Doumergue; again the socialists refused to support this cabinet. As the right wing extremist groups organized themselves as parties in 1935 the radicals, socialists and communists agreed on a 'Popular Front' at the end of 1935.

The electoral victory of the Popular Front in May, 1936 signified the defeat of French right wing authoritarianism. Léon Blum's cabinet consisted of socialist and radical ministers and enjoyed initially the support of the communists as well (Jackson 1988, 6-9). It embarked on a series of important social policy reforms. Although the Popular Front by no means managed to bring overall stability into French politics, this period signified a relative calm. The last years before the war entailed renewed economic and currency problems as well as disagreements over defense spendings and foreign policy strategies.

Belgium

Belgium's march toward democracy started immediately after the proclamation of Belgian independence in 1830. The form of government introduced in 1831 was a strictly constitutional and defined the people as the sole source of legitimate state power. Nevertheless, the division of power provided for by the constitution was not in accordance with the rules of parliamentary democracy. In practice, however, the monarch utilized his far-reaching executive powers largely in accordance with parliamentary principles. From the 1880s on, stepwise suffrage extensions as well as a degree of proportional representation were introduced (Mackie and Rose 1991, 39-40; Tingsten 1933, 627-630).

During the world war, a Cabinet of National Unity comprising all three major political forces - the catholics, the liberals and the socialists - was formed. In 1919, a similar government introduced unversal manhood suffrage as well as voting rights for women whose sons or husbands had died during the war. Two years later a general revision of the constitution was carried out. The selection of the members of the Chamber of Deputies would no longer involve a successive series of elections. The elections to the Senate were made strictly democratic. The electoral system was now entirely based on the principle of proportional representation.

Belgian politics revolved around three major dimensions: economy, language and religion. The first cleavage was salient for the Workers' Party, which controlled the mass of the industrial working class vote, mustering almost forty per cent of the total vote in the interwar period. The language issue involved the endeavor to render Flemish equal with French in all spheres of social life. It was politically not as salient as during the post-WWII period, but id did give rise to a Flemish Nationalist Party with some 6-7 per cent of the vote toward the end of the period. The position of the catholic church and the catholic confession was the main dividing line between the Catholic and Liberal Parties; these parties won around 35 and 16 per cent of the vote, respectively. The liberals worked for a secular state and nonconfessional schools, which was opposed by the catholics. The liberals had their strongholds in urban areas, whereas the Catholic Party controlled the bulk of the peasant vote. These differences notwithstanding, a catholic-liberal coalition was the most frequent type of cabinet in Belgium. However, coalitions including the socialists as well occurred several times; several times, socialist participation signalled a cabinet of 'national unity' in the face of crises and exceptional circumstances (Höjer 1946, 63-290).

The mid-1920s were a period of stagnation for the Belgian economy (Goossens, Peters and Pepermans 1988, 290). The socialists made considerable gains in the 1925 elections while the liberals suffered losses. As a result of prolonged negotiations first a catholic-socialist coalition, then a three party coalition of 'national unity' under Henri Jaspar was formed (May 1926). As soon as the economic crisis had been weathered, however, the socialists left the cabinet. The characteristic catholic-liberal coalitions with recurrent reshuffles reigned until the next Cabinet of National Unity in 1935.

The Great Depression had entailed the rise of fascism in Belgium as well as elsewhere. In Belgium, the fascists were characteristically enough divided along linguistic lines. The larger fascist movement were the Rexists under the leadership of Léon Degrelle; they controlled the Francophone right-wing extremism. *Verdinaso* and the VNV represented Flemish fascism. In both movements a strongly antidemocratic and antiparliamentary line prevailed. Initially, they also commanded para-military organizations; these were outlawed in 1934. In 1935, another 'National Unity Cabinet' was formed under van Zeeland in the face of economic and political chaos. In the elections of May, 1936, Degrelle won over eleven per cent of the vote while all major parties suffered losses. The government outlawed Degrelle's 'March on Brussels' in October.

In March, 1937, Degrelle was ready for a final showdown. He persuaded one of the Rexist MPs in Brussels to resign in order to be able to run personally in the by-elections that had to follow. The cabinet responded by a unique move: it decided to let Prime Minister van Zeeland run alone against Degrelle as a candidate of the three major parties. A couple of days before the election, Cardinal van Roey issued his *'coup de crosse'*, a clear statement that condemned the rexists. The result was a spectacular victory for the government: van Zeeland polled 76 per cent of the vote against 19 per cent for Degrelle (five per cent of the votes were blank ballots) (De Meur and Berg-Schlosser 1990, 25-27).

The rexists never recovered from this defeat. Their share of the vote in the 1939 parliamentary elections fell to 4.4 per cent. Apparently, the front ranging from the catholic church to the socialist organizations had signified the definite demise of authoritarianism in Belgium. For the remainder of the interwar era, Belgian domestic politics returned to 'business as usual'. At the same time, the mounting threat from Germany was felt ever more clearly, binding Belgium closer to France in matters of national defense and rendering fascist and national socialist ideas increasingly suspect in the eyes of Belgian citizens

(Schephens 1980, 505-514).

The Netherlands

The development of Dutch democracy took place between 1848 and 1919. The first year marks the introduction of representative government, the second the extension of suffrage to women. Between these years, a fairly steady expansion toward fully-fledged democracy can be discerned: 1887, 1896 and 1917 mark important suffrage extensions.

Somewhat paradoxically, it was a formally non-political wartime (1914-18) cabinet under Cort van der Linden that introduced the constitutional reform which completed the process of democratization in the Netherlands. Along with universal suffrage for men as well as for women, proportional representation was introduced to replace the old system with single member constituencies and two ballots. The same reform brought a solution to one of the most complicated problems in Dutch politics, which for many years had rendered inter-party cooperation difficult: the question of public versus private schools.

The complications attached to the school issue reflected one of the basic cleavages in Dutch politics: religion. It conditioned social and political life, including the formation of the party system, to a decisive degree. The Liberal Party represented the secularized segments of urban Holland. The Anti-Revolutionary Party represented the opposite standpoint of the Reformed Church and the Catholic Party that of the catholic population. The Christian Historical Party, a splinter from the Liberal Party, normally sided with these two main religious parties against the liberals. Up until the world war the Social Democratic League remained more or less a *quantité négligeable* in Dutch politics (Goudsblom, 1967, 82-94).

Nevertheless, the catchwords for interwar Dutch politics are stability and consensus, especially if the development is compared to that in other European countries. The party system as well as the numerical strength of the various parties displayed remarkable continuity over the period. For instance, between 1922 and 1937 the largest party, the Catholic People's Party, polled between 27.9 and 29.9 per cent of the vote in five consecutive elections (Mackie and

Rose 1991, 17.4b). Similarly, the fairly large number of cabinets should not conceal the fact that there was an extraordinary degree of continuity in terms of cabinet personnel. Between 1918 and 1939, there were ten different cabinets but only three different prime ministers; more than half of this time, Henrik Colijn of the Anti-Revolutionary Party was Prime Minister (Regenten und Regierungen, 353-354). The mechanism greated for labor market questions (*Hoge Raad voor Arbeid*) meant that a lot of the potential political tension created by labor market disputes could be discussed in direct and continued deliberations between employer and employee organizations and social and economic policy experts (Aarebrot 1991, 3). Moreover, the segmentation of Dutch society entailed a decentralized decision-making process in many fields of social life (Gladdish 1991, 27-29).

The Great Depression nevertheless created noticeable political unrest. The appearance of the NSB, the national socialist movement, in 1931, was the first sign; at the height of its success, the NSB polled eight per cent of the vote in the 1935 provincial elections. Moreover, in 1933 the communists doubled their representation in the *Tweede Kameer*, although they still commanded merely four seats. The government responded promptly by introducing a legislation prohibiting political uniforms and disbanding the WA, the national socialist militia. Moreover, public servants were forbidden to join 'organizations that were considered subversive', in practice communist and national socialist organizations (Aarebrot 1991, 6). An increasing number of social, political and religious organizations also renounced national socialism. At the same time, the expansionist Keynesian economic policies introduced by the government served to alleviate the economic hardships of large groups of employees and farmers. During the second half of the 1930s, a widespread fear of German expansionism made it increasingly difficult for national socialists to appeal to the Dutch opinion (van der Wusten and Smit 1980, 538-540). Perhaps more than anywhere else in Europe, the threat from Germany fostered national unity and political moderation in the Netherlands.

Switzerland

Switzerland is a case apart in the family of democratic nations in Europe. The combination of federalism, plebiscitary democracy and a policy of strict neutrality in external relations give the country a special profile as a political system. Moreover, the history of Swiss democracy is also rather peculiar, even extreme in a certain sense. On the one hand, Switzerland belongs to the very early democratizers: universal suffrage to all male citizens aged twenty or over was introduced in 1848, simultaneously with the creation of the modern Federal State of Switzerland. On the other hand, women had to wait until 1971 for the right to vote (Mackie and Rose 1991, 421-422).

Swiss parliamentarism also has peculiar features. The bicameral legislature, the Federal Assembly, has, to be sure, a composition which is quite normal for a federal state. The Council of States consists of the representatives of the cantons elected in various ways determined by the individual cantons. The National Council consists of representatives chosen by the people in direct elections in each canton. What is special is the executive. The cabinet, the Federal Council, is elected after each parliamentary election by the Federal Assembly. It sits throughout the parliamentary period, and its composition is basically a direct reflection of the party constellations in the parliament. The prime minister, or the President of the Federal Council, is elected annually among its members; his role is to be chairman of the council and to represent it, but he does not have the same status as prime ministers in other parliamentary systems. Moreover, the council lacks the right to dissolve the parliament. Nevertheless, the Federal Council occupies a central position in the legislative work at the federal level (Codding 1965, 69-85).

The Swiss party system underwent a change as a consequence of the introduction of proportional representation in 1919. At the same time, the fundamental disagreements between the parties over the status of the federation had all but disappeared. Moreover, the reform was followed by a dramatic increase in turnout, from some fifty per cent to around eighty per cent in 1919. The three traditional parties - catholic conservatives, radical democrats and liberal conservatives - had to face competition from the social democrats and a new 'Farmers, Traders and Citizens' Party'. For the Liberal Conservatives this competition entailed a marginalization, and the Radical Democrats also lost almost half of their seats between 1917 and 1919. The constellations became, however, stable in a matter of a few years, and the Swiss party system in the interwar period displays a high degree of stability

(Ruffieux 1983, 154-155; Tingsten 1933, 622-627; Mackie and Rose 1991, 430-433).

The 1919 election also marked the growing importance of 'normal' socio-economic issues in Swiss politics. Religious and constitutional questions had lost much of their importance, and the socialist-nonsocialist cleavage had become increasingly salient as the central dividing line. The social democrats long perceived of themselves as 'outsiders' in the political system; up until 1929, for instance, they on principle rejected participation in the Federal Council.

Political extremism was weak in Switzerland throughout the period. The communists reached their highest share of the vote in 1939, which gave them four out of 194 seats in the National Council. The crisis of the 1930s also entailed a fascist current, which was especially embodied in the National Front, a national socialist movement. Due to the federal and multicultural structure of the Swiss state, the Germanophile profile of the Front made it impossible for the movement to gain national significance. Just as many other countries, Switzerland feared the growing militancy of Hitler's Germany. The National Front did gain a seat in the National Council in 1935; its all time high was 0.5 per cent of the vote, indicating that fascism could scarcely threaten the fundamental stability of Swiss democracy (Glaus 1980, 467-478).

Czechoslovakia

The Czechoslovakian state which was established after the collapse of the Austro-Hungarian empire in 1918 was one of the most genuinely multi-national and multicultural states in Europe. Besides the largest nationalities - the Czechs, the Sudeten-Germans and the Slovaks - there were large groups of Hungarians, Ruthenians, Poles and Jews (Mlynarik 1989, 90). In addition to the ethno-linguistic divisions, religious cleavages, especially that between hussite Czechs and catholic Slovaks were of importance. Along with the cultural differences went the economic and regional cleavages: Bohemia belonged to the heartland of industrial Europe, whereas Slovakia and Ruthenia were highly agrarian (Stone 1989, 2-3; Hapala 1968, 125, 138-139).

The constitution of 1920, as well as much of interwar Czechoslovakian politics, bore the mark of Tomas Masaryk, the founding father of the Czechoslovak state and its longtime (1918-1935) President (Táborsky 1968, 117-119). The constitution established a parliamentary democracy based on a bicameral legislature, the National Assembly, elected through a strictly proportional voting system. The lower house, the Chamber of Deputies, had 300 members elected for a six-year term. Universal suffrage for all adult citizens applied. All men and women aged 26 or over could participate in the elections to the senate, the upper house of the parliament. The senate had, however, only a limited veto power vis-à-vis the Chamber of Deputies. The President of the Republic was chosen by the two houses of the parliament for a seven-year term. His powers were formally fairly limited, the right to dissolve the parliament and call for new elections being his most powerful instrument; thanks to his personal prestige, however, Masaryk as President exerted influence far beyond the formal confines of the presidency (Tingsten 1933, 649-651).

Czechoslovakian politics was as complicated as the country's social structure. Not only were the different nationalities represented by their own parties and social associations. Most of them had a more or less fully-fledged 'party system' of their own ranging from left to right. This made for an extremely high number of political parties. At most, something like fifty parties and fractions competed for the seats in the National Assembly. Among the largest parties were originally the Czech and German social democratic parties and Czech 'National Socialists' (a national party with a radical line in socio-economic matters; it had nothing to do with national socialism of the German variety). A conservative-catholic party led by Father Andrej Hlinka was the largest representative of the Slovak population (Hapala 1968, 125-132). The turnover of cabinets was also considerable: between 1920 and 1938 there were sixteen different cabinets in Czechoslovakia.

Despite the complicated social and political composition of the Czechoslovakian society, the democratic process functioned reasonably well. In terms of political patterns, interwar Czechoslovak history could perhaps be divided into four periods. From the first election in 1918 up until 1926, various Czech coalitions held executive power. In October 1926, the Czech Agrarian Party leader Antonin Svehla formed a cabinet which was supported by most of the nonsocialist parties. Among the ministers there were representatives of German Agrarian and Christian Social Parties as well as two Slovaks. This signified a basic consensus across the most important ethnic divides in Czechoslovak society. This coalition was in 1929 followed by a third type of cabinet, signalling yet another phase in the political development. Franz Udrzal formed a cabinet where German and Czech socialists cooperated with Slovaks as well as with German and Czech centrist parties (Bruegel 1973, 74-85; Tingsten 1933, 652-654).

The final phase of Czechoslovakian political development largely starts with Hitler's rise to power in Germany in 1933. From that year on, K. Henlein's national socialist party in the Sudetenland rapidly gained momentum. It tuned to the German propaganda and became openly separatist (Bruegel 1973, 110-146; Mlynárik 1989, 93-95) Representatives of the German population continued to participate in cabinets throughout the 1930s, but their support dwindled; in the 1938 regional elections, Henlein's national socialists already polled over ninety per cent of the Sudeten-German vote. Meanwhile, Hlinka's Slovak National Party had also become openly fascist and separatist in its orientation.

Despite these growing difficulties and extremist tendencies, largely supported and fomented by Germany, the definite collapse of Czechoslovakian democracy only resulted from the direct German intervention under the Munich Treaty. Thus, as a democratic system interwar Czechoslovakia must be regarded as one of the 'survivors'. In the 1920s it created a relatively stable system for the democratic representation of the various groups in the country. Basically, this system continued to work beyond the Great Depression, and it took a foreign intervention to put an end to it.

Denmark

The process of democratization in Denmark, which started with the introduction of a progressive constitutional rule in 1848, suffered somewhat of a setback in 1866. That year, a constitutional revision confirmed the formal authority of the King over administration and foreign policy as well as his legislative powers and his right to dissolve the parliament. The comparatively liberal suffrage rules remained in force, however, creating a tension between the increasingly democratic parliament and the conservative executive. Toward the end of the 19th Century, the democratically oriented Liberal Party (*Venstre*) found and ally in the social democrats. In 1901 the King had no choice but to appoint a liberal Prime Minister; this signified the breakthrough of parliamentarism. The process of democratization continued unabated during the world war (Denmark remained neutral): in 1915 universal suffrage for men and women was introduced. The introduction of proportional representation added the final characteristic feature to the Danish political system in 1920 (Miller 1991, 25-27).

By the beginning of the 1920s, the Danish party system and the basic parliamentary constellations had been established. The Liberal Party had been divided into an Agrarian Party (which retained the old party name, *Venstre*) and the Radical Liberal Party. The Social Democratic Party had excluded its youth organization, which had criticized the party for its cooperation with the radical liberals. The youth organization went on to form the Danish Communist Party in 1919. The conservatives were the main party on the right. In terms of electoral support, the social democrats and *Venstre* were the main parties during the interwar period. In 1920, they both polled about one-third of the vote. In the course of the period, however, the social democrats grew rapidly to more than forty per cent, whereas *Venstre* lost half of its vote, being about equal in size to the conservatives. The radical liberals won about ten per cent of the vote, whereas the communists remained insignificant with one or two per cent of the electorate behind them (Berglund and Lindström 1978, 26-70, 82-83).

Compared to most of interwar Europe, Danish politics was stable and rather devoid of dramatic ingredients. Two basic coalitions reigned throughout the period. Agrarian cabinets which could rely on the support of the conservatives alternated with social democratic cabinets either based on cooperation with the radical liberals (1924-26) or with direct participation of radical liberal ministers (1929-39) (Berglund and Lindström 1978, 145). Nevertheless, the Great Depression entailed severe economic problems requiring special political solutions in Denmark as well. Although anti-system parties and movements at all times remained peripheral in Denmark, the 1930s witnessed the activation of a national socialist movement and a clear growth in the communist vote as well. In January 1933, the legendary social democratic Prime Minister Thorvald Stauning struck a much publicized deal on a package of crisis policies with the Agrarian *Venstre* Party. This was to be the first in a series of 'Red-Green' agreements in Scandinavia; it signalled a basic democratic consensus among the main parties in the face of economic turbulence and extremist challenges against the democratic form of government (Lindström 1985, 155-177; Karvonen 1991 A, 55-58).

Sweden

Sweden belongs to the late democratizers among the West European nations. The 1866 Representative Reform, which finally abolished the Diet based on the Four Estates, provided for a constitutional rule but was a far cry from a system based on mass democracy. The executive power remained firmly in the hands of the monarch, and suffrage to the two-chamber *Riksdag* was severely limited. As late as in 1905, merely some thirty per cent of adult male citizens had the right to vote. Moreover, turnout remained low, being merely forty per cent toward the end of the 19th Century (Tingsten 1933, 570-577).

From the 1890s on, the liberals and the social democrats (the SAP) joined forces to establish democracy and parliamentarism in the country. The 1907 electoral reform did away with the property requirement for the franchise and introduced proportional representation. Ten years later, the principle of parliamentarism started to function. Finally the 1918-21 constitutional revision entailed a complete democratization of the elections to the first as well as to the second chamber; women as well as men were now given the right to vote (Mackie and Rose 1991, 400-401).

The Swedish party system in the interwar period is characterized by a growing social democracy (SAP) which rapidly becomes considerably larger than any other party. Equally conspicuous is the shrinking liberal share of the party spectrum. The liberals suffered from party splits and polled merely around twelve per cent of the vote in the late 1930s, about half of their share fifteen years earlier. A relatively stable Conservative Party and a sizable Agrarian party are other typical features. The Communist Party, a result of the split of the Social Democratic Labor Party in 1917, was at all times dwarfed by the reformist party. Nevertheless, it was not entirely a *quantité négligeable*: in 1928, it managed to poll 6.4 per cent of the vote (Berglund and Lindström 1978, 85).

Interwar Swedish politics, especially the 1920s, was a period of minority parliamentarism. The social democrats, the liberals and the conservatives took turns to form minority cabinets. Especially in the 1920s, these had to rely on temporary majorities created around individual issues in the parliament (Stjernquist 1966, 121-122). Coalition cabinets were not practised. The social democrats, who were rather moderate in cabinet position, had fairly far-reaching socialist programs which effectively pre-empted more permanent cooperation across the socialist-nonsocialist divide. In 1928, after an election campaign which was characterized by rather doctrinaire socialist demands on the part of the social democrats and conservative accusations against the SAP for 'bolshevism', the social democrats met with their hitherto greatest electoral disaster. This caused the SAP to gradually shift to a more moderate posture; party leader P.A. Hansson's famous phrase about the 'People's Home' is the classic example of this reorientation (Karvonen 1991 A, 58-64). In May 1933, in the midst of the Great Depression, the SAP and the Agrarian Party reach an agreement on a massive package of anti-depression policies especially designed to meet the needs of the workers and the farmers. The deal was preceded by unprecedented compromises on the part of the social democrats and by somewhat of a palace revolution in the Agrarian Party (Lewin 1984, 180-184; Lindström 1985, 159-170). A few years later, the two parties even joined forces in a coalition cabinet which was the only majority cabinet in interwar Swedish history. The deal was not only an agreement on economic and social policies. Equally important, it was an agreement by two major parties that expressedly condemned the anti-democratic tendencies discernible on the left as well as on the right wing. Consequently, fascism never came close to gaining parliamentary representation in Sweden, and communist representation was down to about half of its all-time high by the mid-1930s.

Norway

When Norway became a kingdom under the Swedish crown in 1814, a strangely dual situation was created from the constitutional point of view. The constitution adopted for Norway that year belonged to the most progressive in entire Europe. Simultaneously, executive power lay in the hands of the Swedish monarch, who represented one of the most dated systems. A major part of Norwegian constitutional history in the 19th Century involves a struggle between the basically unicameral *Storting* and the monarch's attempts to hold back the development toward mass democracy. Toward the end of the century the struggle for democratization increasingly coincided with a struggle for independence from Sweden. This process entailed important suffrage extensions in 1884 and 1898. In 1884 the King was for the first time compelled to appoint a liberal cabinet according to the wishes of the parliament. In 1905 the union with Sweden was dissolved, and Norway became a completely independent constitutional monarchy with a parliamentary system of government. At the same time, the indirect electoral system used hitherto was replaced by a direct system of elections. In 1913, suffrage was extended to all adult women as well and in 1919 a proportional voting method replaced the majoritarian electoral system (Arntzen and Knudsen 1981, 16-18).

Norwegian social democracy (DNA) had been one of the major actors in the front for independence and democracy. It had cooperated with the liberals in particular on these issues. After 1905, however, this cooperation was replaced by a confrontation due to divergencies on a number of important political and economic issues. Between 1905 and 1918, therefore, the social democratic role in Norwegian politics was that of a bystander. This period was an important precondition of the social democratic decision to seek entry into the Comintern in 1919. The DNA withdrew from the Comintern four years later. The disagreement over this decision ended in a party split, whereby the Comintern wing of the party formed the Norwegian Communist Party. Moreover, the outspoken reformists had also left the DNA, which, even after the break with the Comintern wing, defined itself as a communist party. The 1927 party congress brought the reformists back to the DNA ranks, but the radical image of Norwegian social democracy persisted well into the 1930s (Furre 1972, 124 ff.)

This being the case, there was little potential for cooperation with the nonsocialist parties. Throughout the 1920s, in fact, Norway was a politically polarized society. The liberals (17-20 per cent of the vote), conservatives (20-30 per cent) and the agrarians (10-15 per cent) took turns to form minority cabinets. The social democrats doubled their vote after the party unification in 1927, gaining about 36 per cent of the total vote. They were subsequently given a chance to form a cabinet in January, 1928. The program of this cabinet led by Chr. Hornsrud flatly stated that the objective of the DNA was to achieve a socialist society in Norway. The conservatives, liberals and agrarians joined forces against what they described as a 'class government' and threw Hornsrud out of office after merely a couple of weeks. The 'maximalist' tendencies in the DNA again gained momentum. This was witnessed in the 1930 party program, which was quite doctrinaire in its marxist orientation. The bourgeois parties made use of this in their 1930 election campaign accusing the DNA for a 'Russian orientation', and gave the social democrats a serious electoral setback. When the Great Depression hit Norway there seemed to be little potential for a political consensus in the country (Ryssevik 1991, 15-45; Karvonen 1991 A, 64-69).

The following years were a period of intense ideological debate within the DNA. No definite consensus ensued, but the 1933 election campaign was carried out under conspicuously moderate and even populist devices. The response of the electorate was favorable, giving the DNA for the first time more than forty per cent of the vote. Meanwhile, the parliamentary group of the DNA led by Johan Nygaardsvold carried out negotiations on possible coalitions. In March 1935, Nygaardsvold managed to strike a deal with the Agrarian Party on a series of crisis measures. A few days later he formed a social democratic cabinet that was to sit until the outbreak of the war.

The 'red-green' agreement between the social democrats and the agrarians naturally centered around economic and social policy reforms. Nevertheless, there was also a concern for political extremism among the social democrats and the agrarians. There was considerable extreme right wing activity in Norway, and the social democrats had experience of sizable communist opposition. Again, therefore, the 'red-green' deal was as much a signal of a new democratic consensus as it was a social and economic policy innovation (Lindström 1985, 155-177).

Finland

After some six hundred years as part of the Kingdom of Sweden, Finland was ceded to Russia in 1809. It was granted a far-reaching autonomy and the right to maintain its Swedish laws and social order. From the point of view of democratization, most of the 'autonomy period' (1809-1917) entailed almost total stagnation. In 1906 - as a result of the defeat in the Russo-Japanese war and the 1905 Russian Revolution - the czar was finally compelled to give in to the growing demands for democratization. The 1906 Representative Reform over night replaced the *last* system based on the four estates in Northern Europe by the *first* parliament based on universal suffrage in entire Europe (Alapuro 1988, 114-118).

As in Norway, the struggle for democracy had been part of a fight for national existence; since the 1880s, the Finnish autonomy had been subjected to growing pressures on the part of Russian nationalists and the central government. Quite like in Norway, moreover, the alliance between social democrats and liberals became increasingly uneasy after 1906, partly due to the rapid electoral gains of the former. Moreover, the lack of parliamentarism - the Czar could still appoint cabinets at will - made the work of the unicameral legislature frustrating. The 1917 revolutions in Russia created a power vacuum which was utilized to declare Finland independent in December, 1917. Shortly thereafter, the revolutionary wing of the Social Democratic Party (SDP) took to arms in an attempt at a revolution.

The 1918 civil war was a victory for the bourgeois 'Whites'. Shortly after the war, the defeated 'Reds' split up in reformist social democrats and a revolutionary Communist Party. The attempt of the conservatives and the Swedish Party to introduce a monarchy failed; instead, the 1919 Form of Government provided for a dualistic system, in which parliamentarism was combined with a presidency with far-reaching powers including foreign policy leadership, the right to appoint cabinets and the right to dissolve the parliament (Mohlin 1987, 27-47; Anckar 1987, 57-65).

After the Civil War, Finland was a politically divided society. The Left, now divided into reformist social democracy and revolutionary communism, was viewed with suspicion by the nonsocialist groups. The nonsocialists were internally divided as well. Besides the 'normal' rivalry between conservative, liberal and agrarian parties the linguistic issue complicated political cooperation; in the 1920s, the relations between the Finnish majority and the Swedish minority grew increasingly tense (Hämäläinen 1966). As none of the parties was anywhere near a parliamentary majority of its own, the 1920s became a period of minority parliamentarism with numerous cabinet crises. At the same time, the communists, who controlled most of the labor unions, went in for a militant strategy which, i.a., produced prolonged strike waves toward the end of the 1920s (Karvonen 1988, 17-18).

The emergence of the anti-communist Lapua Movement in late 1929 signified a new period in Finnish politics. Lapua rapidly gained momentum and managed to push an anticommunist legislation through parliament in 1930. It was something of a central actor in Finnish politics in the early 1930s, influencing cabinet formations and presidential elections to a decisive degree. With these initial successes the movement rapidly grew more militant and took on an increasingly clear fascist character. In February, 1932, it got involved in what looked like an attempt at a coup d'etat ('the Mäntsälä Revolt'). President P.E. Svinhufvud, thus far sympathetic to the movement, resolutely intervened. Lapua was declared illegal and its leaders were arrested; shortly thereafter, however, a fascist party (IKL) was established to carry on Lapua's activities (Rintala 1962, 164-220).

As the economic situation had deteriorated and the fascist threat become increasingly acute, the centrist parties had drifted further away from the conservatives; the latter persistently gave their support to Lapua even after the Mäntsälä Revolt. Between 1932 and 1936, a liberal minority cabinet governed with the tacit support of the social democrats; the SDP wished to keep the Lapua-oriented conservatives out of government. The Agrarian Party, which had emerged as the second largest party right after the SDP, grew increasingly dissatisfied with the crisis policies of the liberals. In September 1936, they reached a compromise with the social democrats on a package of social and economic policies. In early 1937 they joined forces to elect Agrarian K. Kallio to the presidency. Kallio promptly proceeded to appoint the first 'red-green' cabinet in the history of independent Finland. In terms of its parliamentary base, this cabinet was stronger than any previous cabinet. Besides social and economic reforms, its program clearly declared the defense of democracy against extremism as a central goal. The 'red-green' compromise therefore brought much needed stability into the parliamentary scene, while at the same time signalling the definite defeat of the extreme right in Finnish politics (Karvonen 1991 A, 70-75).

Some concluding points

A snapshot of Europe at the beginning of the 1920s shows a politically largely homogeneous region with a high degree of optimism as concerns the future of democracy. Roughly fifteen years later, the eye of the camera would have caught an entirely different view. The democratic structures that were common throughout Europe after the world war had widely varying roots in the histories of individual countries. Democratic mechanisms were differently constructed and they functioned differently in different societies; in a word, democracy *meant* a wide variety of this to the various peoples of Europe. With the benefit of this hindsight, it is perhaps no wonder that it met with different degrees of success in different national contexts.

At the same time, historical background apparently does not offer a clear-cut explanation of the course of interwar European politics. In fact, looking at the end result - the breakdown or survival of democracy - a number of patterns can be discerned. Some of them seem rather intriguing given the similarities and differences in historical background.

The early democratizers of Western Europe - countries where democracy was introduced stepwise over a long period of time - form a distinct group of 'survivors'. England, France, Belgium, the Netherlands, Switzerland, Denmark and Norway surely belong to this group (Sweden in many ways, too, but she can hardly be called an early democratizer). Italy forms the conspicuous exception here.

The four other cases of 'breakdown' in our sample - Germany, Austria, Latvia and Estonia - are all late democratizers. Together with the observation above, this certainly forms a pattern of considerable interest. Nevertheless, it should not be overlooked that the cases of Czechoslovakia and Finland clearly contradict this pattern. In fact, it is not only the late and sudden process of democratization that is common to these states. Basically, they all (including Germany as a political system) emerged from the WWI settlement. Moreover, the similarities between Latvia and Czechoslovakia on the one hand, and those between Estonia and Finland on the other are intriguing. Czechoslovakia and Latvia share the high degree of ethnic segmentation as well as an extremely fractionaliozed party system. Still only the latter experienced a breakdown of democracy in the interwar period. Finland and Estonia both emerged as independent states from the collapse of the Russian Empire. They went through a civil war/liberation war, where 'white' nationalists fought against Russian bolsheviks as well as against indigenous revolutionary socialists. They both experienced strong right wing nationalist/fascist currents, in which the role of 'white' civil war veterans was central. Moreover, one may feel tempted also to point to the geographic proximity and linguistic affinity between the two states. Nevertheless, democracy went under only in Estonia.

As for the four Scandinavian countries, the similarities in the political responses to the crisis of the 1930s are striking. A 'red-green' compromise between social democratic and agrarian parties was reached in all countries. Especially for Finland, but also for Norway, this marked a clear shift from earlier confrontationist politics to a more consensus-oriented political climate. Elsewhere (Karvonen and Lindström 1988, Karvonen 1991) we have discussed the dynamics of this Scandinavian development in greater detail (see also Lindström 1985, 155-177). Here, it should be pointed out that Czechoslovakian politics in the interwar era also to a large extent rested on a 'red-green' consensus between social democrats and agrarians (Luebbert 1991, 292-294).

The formation of more or less unorthodox coalitions was, however, by no means a Scandinavian specialty. With varying degrees of novelty, the Great Depression and the fascist threat gave rise to coalitions in England, France, the Netherlands and in Belgium.

Several countries came close to a coup d'etat or an authoritarian takeover. In France and in Finland this was indeed a vivid possibility; the Belgian case was perhaps not equally dramatic, but a confrontation between fascism and the democratic forces took on the character of an open showdown here as well. All this goes to say that the details of these events as compared to successful cases of authoritarian takeover stand out as questions of paramount importance for further study.

Finally, authoritarianism itself had varying political backgrounds in the five cases of breakdown. Italy and Germany of course represent clear-cut cases of fascist takeover. In Austria, Latvia and especially in Estonia countering the fascist threat was one of the main motives for those politicians who effectuated the transition from democratic rule. In Austria, Dollfuss wished to combat national socialism as much as social democracy; during the Dollfuss-Schuschnigg regime, however, fascism of the *Heimwehr* variety increasingly set its mark on the Austrian regime. Similarly, Latvia under Ulmanis clearly moved in the direction of a fascist-inspired corporatist system. As for Estonia it would be to stretch the concept of fascism much too far to brand the Päts regime as a fascist one.

In sum, this bird's eye view of interwar European politics points to some mechanisms of obvious importance for the viability of democracy. At the same time, it is clear that no simple, clear-cut rule emerges from our descriptive account. It seems warranted to inquire into the dynamics of the interwar crisis in a more rigorous and systematic manner.

Chapter 3

Fragmentation, Stability and Breakdown

This chapter examines the empirical relationship between party system characteristics, cabinet stability and the fate of pluralist democracy in interwar Europe. Its main objective is to test basic notions in a literature which has been characterized by Lawrence Mayer (1980 B, 335) in the following manner:

> The collapse of parliamentary democracies in Europe prior to World War II generated a search for the internal weakness of such systems. Out of this search came a suggestion from several quarters that multiparty parliamentary democracies were more prone to cabinet instability than were two-party systems. Parliamentary democracies, beset with such cabinet instability, cannot govern effectively. Therefore, it was suggested, such instable systems were readily replaced by more authoritarian political regimes that appeared better able to provide for the efficient functioning of that system.

There are three elements in this view of democratic systems: the degree of *fragmentation of the party system*, the *stability of cabinets* and the eventual *breakdown or survival of democracy*. The latter is of course to be regarded as the effect or the dependent variable, whereas party system fragmentation and cabinet instability constitute causes or independent variables. The basic aim of the present chapter is to find out whether these three factors were in fact interrelated in interwar Europe.

In the 'theory' succintly described by Mayer above, the fragmentation of the party system is the basic explanatory factor, whereas cabinet instability is a step on the way toward the breakdown of democracy. The chain of causality is therefore expected to be as follows:

Fragmentation ---> Cabinet instability ---> Breakdown

Here, however, this model is 'used rather than believed'. *A priori*, several combinations of these three factors seem to make sense:

Table 1. Possible relationships between fragmentation, instability and breakdown

		Cabinet instability			
		Low		High	
		Breakdown?			
		No	Yes	No	Yes
	Low	1	2	3	4
Frag-ment-ation					
	High	5	6	7	8

Cases 1 and 8 represent the paradigmatic types: 'the stable two-party system that survived' and 'the unstable fragmented system that went under'. Type 2 might, for instance, depict a situation where a dominant party reinforces its position by starting to rule in a more authoritarian fashion. Types 3, 4 and 6 may seem unlikely at first glance. Still it is imaginable that there are formally democratic states in which the real power center lies outside the democratic institutions. Whether democracy is allowed to continue functioning or is replaced by an authoritarian regime depends on these factors (e.g., the armed forces). In a word, politics is *secondary* in these states. Type 5 might then be the 'consociational democracy' with a high degree of party system fragmentation combined with stable governments and a continued democratic regime; here, power-sharing through cabinet functions as a channel through which the fragmented political interests are reconciled. Type 7, finally, defies the basic chain of causality by displaying high levels of party system fragmentation as well as cabinet instability without a subsequent breakdown of democracy. It is here that we would expect to find various 'crisis coalitions', i.e. realignments between the parties in the face of a threat against democracy itself. Such coalitions may provide for increased cabinet stability but may just as well be transient and simply help the system weather the acute crisis. A quite different solution might be that a system responds to a crisis by a rapid succession of cabinets that provide the various parties access to governmental power, thus preventing the 'ghettoization' of any part of the party spectrum. This is similar to the paradox of 'stable instability' (Taylor and Herman 1971, 29), a situation in which government instability functions as a safety valve for the survival of the democratic system itself.

All this goes to say that we should not only try to determine statistical correlations between fragmentation measures, stability and breakdown, although this certainly is the natural first step. It is equally important to try to determine the *circumstances* under which party system fragmentation bred cabinet instability and paved the way for an authoritarian takeover, or, conversely, what factors and measures helped some countries overcome the effects of fragmentation and instability. Nevertheless, in this chapter the focus is on the explanatory power of factors related to the party system itself.

Previous research

Relevant previous research can be grouped under three headings: 1. theoretical generalizations about the relationship between party system fragmentation and democratic stability; 2. empirical studies of cabinet stability and party system fragmentation in post-WWII democracies; 3. empirical studies of party system characteristics and democratic stability in the interwar period.

As mentioned above in Chapter 1, the early theorizing about the relationship between party systems and democratic stability is largely associated with F.A. Hermens. Both his original propositions and some of the work of his contemporaries were surveyed in that part of the book. Here it is sufficient to again note that Hermens' original focus, the relationship between electoral systems and party system fragmentation has been subjected to criticism. In the present analysis, the focus is on the latter part of Hermens' implicit model, the relationship between fragmentation, cabinet stability and the survivability of democratic regimes.

In the early literature, the character of the two-party system was perceived in a rather uncomplicated manner. The idea of party system fragmentation was implicit rather than explicit. The authors simply spoke about 'twopartism' and 'multipartism'; their explanatory factor was a dichotomous one.

In the scholarly debate it was soon found that such a distinction was oversimplified. Not only was 'multipartism' a term which covered a far from homogeneous group of states; it was in fact difficult to find more than a couple of examples of genuine two-party systems (Mayer 1980 B, 336-337; Sartori 1990, 339-340). Clearly, fragmentation must be a matter of degree rather than of kind.

Giovanni Sartori has underlined the importance of the interaction between party system fragmentation and ideological distance for the stability of democracy. In a 1976 study he concludes that

> When a maximal ideological distance engenders a centrifugal competition, a two-party system is either blown up or paves the way to a civil war confrontation... extreme multipartism represents - under conditions of maximal polarization - the most likely outcome and, at the same time, the survival solution (Sartori 1990, 348).

In a study published jointly with Giacomo Sani a decade later, however, Sartori came to a conclusion that does not similarly challenge the very foundation of the early theorizing about twopartism and multipartism. On the basis of an empirical examination of eleven West European states in the 1970s Sani and Sartori conclude that

> Fragmentation handicaps the 'working' of democracy if, and only if, it expresses [ideological] polarization. When it does not, when a polity qualifies as being low on the polarization measures, then a democracy can work even if its party system is fragmented (Sani and Sartori 1985, 335).

A largely similar hypothesis had earlier been presented by Lawrence Dodd, who expected parliaments with party systems that are polarized, fractionalized and unstable to produce governmental instability (Dodd 1976, 68). In both these studies, it is the interaction between ideological polarization and party system fragmentation, rather than any of the variables as such, that is seen as the crucial factor behind instability.

I have earlier argued that the survival of Scandinavian democracy in the interwar years can partly be understood in terms of a specific state of party system fragmentation. In Scandinavia, the fragmentation of the bourgeois parties together with the social democratic dominance on the Left made for a historical compromise between social democrats and agrarians, an agreement which reinforced Scandinavian democracy as well as government stability to a decisive degree (Karvonen and Lindström 1988, 4-8; Karvonen 1989, 27-28, 31-33). Briefly, this argumentation would seem to suggest that it was not fragmentation as such, but the *fragmentation of the left wing* that was problematic from the point of view of democratic stability.

These are some of the theoretical models that seem worth testing besides the simple single-factor explanation found in the early literature. Here, propositions that involve party system fragmentation as an ingredient in more complex multivariate analyses will be omitted, as such analyses can be accomodated by other ongoing projects (Berg-Schlosser 1990; Zimmermann and Saalfeld 1988).

What do we know? Empirical studies

We are faced with something of a paradox as concerns systematic empirical tests of the proposition about party system fragmentation and the stability of democracy. The original theoretical notion was largely based on European politics in the interwar period; most of the empirical work has concerned Western democracies after World War II. There are a couple of important exceptions to this rule; these will be commented at some length below. Before that, some representatives of the more comprehensive research on the postwar period should be presented.

The most frequently cited study is a 1971 article by Michael Taylor and V.M. Herman. Taylor and Herman studied all cabinets (N=196) in all democratic states (N=19) between 1945 and 1969. The unit of analysis was the single cabinet, and a total of thirteen hypotheses about the correlates of cabinet duration were tested empirically against these aggregate figures. Several of the basic ideas in the early literature discussed above found support in these bivariate analyses. The most interesting findings from our point of view were that government stability was found to be negatively correlated (r=-.39) with the number of parties holding seats in parliament and that this correlation was even stronger (r=-.45) when parliamentary fractionalization was measured with Rae's fractionalization index. Moreover, government fractionalization was found to have a similar effect; government stability was found to be negatively correlated (r=-.31) with the number of parties in the government (Taylor and Herman 1971, 30-31). All in all, this study lended reasonable support to the original ideas about the effects of party system fragmentation.

Using a somewhat different measure called the Party Aggregation Index, Lawrence Mayer (1980) studied eighteen democracies during the period 1960-1974. His index not only took into account the number of parties but also the relative strength of the largest party. Mayer used the individual country as the unit of analysis, and found that almost one-third of the variation in cabinet stability was accounted for by his conceptualization of party system aggregation. His conclusion was: 'In a heuristic sense, perhaps F.A Hermens has made a contribution after all' (Mayer 1980 B, 346).

The study which clearly comes closest to our aims is a 1988 article by Ekkart Zimmermann entitled 'The Puzzle of Government Duration. Evidence from Six European Countries during the Interwar Period'. As part of a larger study with the aim of 'substantively understanding why some governments collapsed under the impact of the world economic crisis of the 1930s (or more generally under the challenges during the interwar period) whereas others did not' (p. 353), Zimmermann examines a total of 117 governments in Germany, Austria, France, the United Kingdom, Belgium and the Netherlands in 1919-1938. As in the study by Taylor and Herman, the unit of analysis is the individual cabinet; the explanatory factors tested are largely similar to those used by Taylor and Herman.

Similarly to Taylor and Herman, Zimmermann starts by looking at his empirical material at large in what he calls his 'pooled analysis'. Here, the main results concerning fragmentation go in the same general direction as those of Taylor and Herman, although the correlations are not particularly strong. Thus, both the fractionalization of parliament and the fractionalization of government are found to be negatively related with cabinet stability. Moreover, the left-right variance of parliament (a polarization measure) is found to be negatively related to stability, thus confirming the basic idea of Sani and Sartori about the importance of polarization.

However, Zimmermann also looks at the various correlations for each nation separately ('disaggregated analysis'). Here, the reasonably clear impression from the pooled analysis is replaced by an almost totally incoherent picture. For instance, the correlations between parliament fractionalization and cabinet stability are -.33 (Austria), -.15 (Belgium), .42 (Germany), .01 (Netherlands), -.37 (Britain) and -.16 (France). The corresponding figures for government fractionalization are .08, .28, .31, -.31, .17 and .20. These disaggregated analyses do not seem to indicate any meaningful pattern either countrywise or when the various theoretically derived explanatory factors are grouped together. He finds this highly discomforting and concludes that

> the findings from the pooled analysis - following the tradition in research on parliamentary (and other) correlates of government duration - are misleading if these very same governments are not studied at the level of each individual nation...[T]he need to disaggregate, possibly even after World War II, has been overlooked by researchers (Zimmermann 1988, 353, 355).

One of the most comprehensive works on cabinet durability in general is Lawrence Dodd's 1976 study 'Coalitions in Parliamentary Government'. Its main emphasis is on coalition theory, and Dodd sets out to prove that minimal winning cabinets are the key to governmental stability. To test his thesis, Dodd employs a large number of explanatory factors, including those kinds of fractionalization measures that the studies presented above utilized. What is even more important from our point of view is that the period studied is 1918-1974, and that Dodd presents separate analyses for the interwar and postwar periods. Again, the individual cabinet is the unit of analysis (N=238); seventeen countries are included.

Dodd's study contains most of the empirical material necessary for a test of the basic fragmentation thesis. So much the worse, the reader is left uncertain about the relationship between cabinet durability and party system fragmentation. The reason is that Dodd, instead of using bivariate measures as the other studies, employs composite variables which make it difficult to determine the explanatory power of the individual components. His most powerful explanatory factor for cabinet stability in the interwar period is an interaction score composed of measures for cleavage conflict, parliamentary fractionalization and parliamentary instability: (parliamentary fractionalization x parliamentary instability) x (cleavage conflict). The covariation between this index and government stability is -.54, explaining 29 per cent of the total variation in government stability. What the effect of this *double* multiplicative exercise is on the explanatory power of the individual variables is difficult to determine. The conclusion for the time being must simply be that Dodd's study at least does not serve to refute the thesis about fragmentation and instability.

To sum up: there are several theoretical propositions pertaining to the relationship between fragmentation, instability and breakdown which lend themselves to empirical tests; the empirical evidence mainly gathered from post-WWII democracies lends clear, albeit not overwhelmingly strong support to the basic thesis; systematic empirical research concerning interwar Europe is limited, but points in the same general direction. All in all, it seems warranted to pursue this line of inquiry further in the interwar European context.

Two logics of inquiry

The theoretical starting point for most of the previous empirical studies has been the early literature on party systems (cf. Dodd 1976, 6-10; Mayer 1980 B, 335-336; Taylor and Herman 1971, 28). It could be argued, however, that the systematic quantitative work done by several authors is based on a somewhat different logic than the earlier work. This difference is mainly reflected in the use of individual cabinets rather than countries as the unit of analysis. Zimmermann's emphasis on the importance of analyzing the correlates of cabinet stability within individual countries is the most extreme example (it should be noted, howevere, that Zimmermann does not refer to

Hermens or other early theorists).

The argument about the effects of party system fragmentation originally concerned cross-national comparisons rather than intra-national processes. Fragmented *systems* were expected to be more unstable than non-fragmented ones. This is in fact something quite different than saying that whenever a new party gains a seat in a parliament cabinets in that country are expected to become more unstable according to a certain mathematical formula. The theoretical argument is about fairly static systemic features rather than about a dynamic process of fragmentation. By its nature, therefore, the original theory calls for a comparative design and for aggregate figures. What matters is the country as a whole as compared to other countries: countries tend have a certain, fairly stable, level of fragmentation, which effects the way in which politics is conducted. From a principal point of view, it is less important that such analyses do not easily conform to the requirements of statitistics concerning a sufficiently large number of cases.

Furthermore, if the overall level of fragmentation is generally fairly stable, at least in the sense that one cannot expect the various countries to rank entirely differently from one point in time to another, then intra-nation studies of the kind Zimmermann calls for really do away with the main factor, the crisis itself. The argument in the early literature is not whether there was a linear relationship between fragmentation and instability in a given country; rather, Hermens' implicit argument was that a country at a certain general level of fragmentation tended to become significantly more unstable than a country at a lower level, *once the crisis was a fact* (cf. Hermens 1958, 344-349). The argument is simply that fragmented systems have a poorer capacity for crisis management than non-fragmented ones.

If we shift our focus to processes within individual nations, by contrast, we are not primarily interested in general levels of fragmentation but in *relative changes* in fragmentation, irrespective of whether the starting point is low or high fragmentation.

A fictitious example may illustrate the two different logics. For the sake of the argument, let us think of two countries with varying levels of party system fragmentation and political stability over time. As of about 1930, both countries are hit hard by the Great Depression. Country A has over a long period had a high level of fragmentation and a relatively low level of cabinet stability, whereas B has a low level of fragmentation and a high level of stability. The fragmentation levels remain roughly stable in the course of the crisis, whereas the levels of government stability drop for both countries, reaching almost a state of chaos for A.

Figure 2. Party system fragmentation and cabinet stability in two countries. A fictitious example.

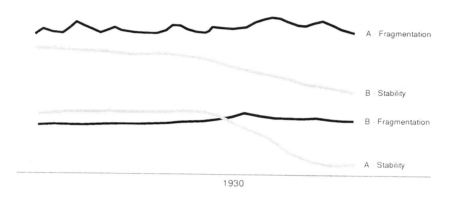

1930

In terms of statistical correlations *within* the countries, there is a *decreasing* degree of association between fragmentation and stability in this example. Following Hermens, however, the end result (the 'final level of stability') when comparing the two *countries* would still be explicable in terms of the general level of fragmentation in them.

The above example is of course somewhat extreme. In real-world situations, studies using cabinets as units of analysis may well reach the same conclusions as studies which are based on data at the level of countries. Nevertheless, the basic difference in the logic of inquiry remains. The early theoretical work concerned the effects of *overall levels* of fragmentation; later systematic analyses, especially Zimmermann's article, pay attention to the *relative changes* in party system fragmentation. To the extent that studies using individual cabinets as units of analysis aim at explaining the ultimate fate of democracy in a cross-national perspective, these cabinet-level data must in fact be aggregated and treated as system level variables; the breakdown or survival of democracy is a system level property (cf. Przeworski and Teune 1970, 49).

At face value, however, both logics seem quite reasonable. This suggests that our empirical analysis should pay attention to *both* of these modes of inquiry. Consequently, the empirical analysis below will be structured according to the following basic questions:

1 Did countries with various levels of party system fragmentation display different levels of cabinet instability, and did this fragmentation and instability explain the ultimate fate of democracy in the interwar period?

2 Did changes in the relative degree of party system fragmentation in individual countries give rise to increased cabinet instability and thus affect the final oucome, i.e., the survival or demise of democratic rule?

These two queries require different methods of analysis. The first question calls for a cross-national examination at aggregate level. The second one involves a separate time-series analysis for each case. It is natural, therefore, to address these questions in two separate sections of this chapter.

Data

Besides the assessment concerning the survival or breakdown of democracy which was made above, the empirical analysis in this chapter concerns party systems and the stability of governments. On both points, conventional definitions guided the selection of data. 'Party systems' simply denote the configurations of parties *holding seats in parliament* in the various countries at various points in time. Strictly speaking, the 'party system' may also include small parties not represented in parliament. It would be next to impossible, however, to find reliable and comprehensive data on such parties from the interwar era for as heterogeneous a group of countries as those in our sample.

Similarly, our definition of 'cabinet stability' is a conventional one. *Cabinet duration measured in days* is used as an indicator of stability. This is hardly a perfect solution (if such a solution exists), and it has received criticism from several authors (cf. Lijphart 1984, 112-113; Mayer 1980 B, 340-341). Still, it remains more straightforward than any weighted index proposed as an alternative (Browne, Frendeis and Gleiber 1986, 93-109; Mayer 1980 B, 340-342). The relative weight assigned to various kinds of cabinet dissolutions in these indices always contains an arbitrary element, which easily conceals cultural biases.

The basic data source concerning party systems, i.e., parliaments, is Thomas T. Mackie nad Richard Rose, *The International Almanac of Electoral History* (1974 edition). This is beyond doubt the most authoritative source as concerns elections and parliaments in the Western World. Three of the countries in our sample are not, however, covered by the Almanac. For Estonia, the data were taken from Artur Mägi, *Das Staatsleben Estlands während seiner Selbständigkeit* (1967). The data on Czechoslovakia were generously provided by Professor John F.D. Bradley. For Latvia, the data originate from Alfreds Bilmanis, *Latvijas Werdegang. Vom Bischofsstaat Terra Mariana bis zur freien Volksrepublik* (1934) and Adolfs Silde, *Latvijas vesture 1914-1940* (1976), sources which were provided by the Center for Baltic Studies at the University of Stockholm.

As for cabinet duration, the data originate from *Regenten und Regierungen der Welt. Teil II: 1492-1953*. This is an authoritative German source which aims at providing systematic and exact information of rulers and governments around the world throughout history. Particular attention is paid to exact dates, including dates for the appointment and resignation of cabinets.

Empirical analysis I: aggregate figures

This section looks for answers to three basic questions:

1 Is the breakdown or survival of democracy explicable in terms of party systemic factors?

2 Is the survival or breakdown of democracy explicable in terms of cabinet

stability?

3 Is cabinet stability explicable in terms of party systemic factors?

As for the main explanatory factors pertaining to party system characteristics, measures of party system fragmentation are at the center of our interest. At the same time, the effects of polarization as well as the fragmentation of the socialist and nonsocialist wings of the party spectrum seem interesting in the light of the previous literature.

Method

The individual country is the unit of analysis employed in this part of our study. The design is cross-national, and the analysis is based on aggregate data.

Sixteen European states are included: Denmark, Finland, Norway, Sweden, Estonia, Belgium, United Kingdom, Germany, France, Austria, Netherlands, Ireland, Switzerland, Italy, Czechoslovakia and Latvia. The criterion for inclusion was that a country must at least for some years have had functioning fully-fledged democratic institutions. Eleven of these countries survived both the first crisis of democracy in the 1920s and the Great Depression of the early and mid-1930s. Authoritarian takeovers took place in Italy (1922), Germany (1933), Austria (1933), Estonia (1934) and Latvia (1934). Consequently, the first dependent variable is dichotomous: democracy either survived or broke down (see Chapter 2).

Cabinet stability appears both as a dependent and an independent variable in this study. Cabinet duration in days is used as an indicator of stability. Average cabinet duration is calculated both for all cabinets and for 'new cabinets', i.e. those which entailed a change of Prime Minister.

Party system characteristics are described in terms of fragmentation and polarization. Fragmentation is measured in terms of the number of parties represented in Parliament, Rae's Index of Fractionalization (F) and Mayer's Party Aggregation index (A). The former index is based on the relative share of the seats held by each party (for a comprehensive discussion, see Taagepera and Soberg Shugart 1988, 79-81).

For the calculation Rae's F the Herfindahl-Hirschman concentration index, or HH is used:

$$HH = \Sigma p^2_i$$

where p_i is the fractional share of the i-th component and Σ stands for the summation over all components. The values of HH can range from 0 to 1: if one component has a 100 per cent share, HH=1.00, if all components are extremely small, HH tends toward zero. The Rae fractionalization index (F) then is the reverse of HH:

$$F = 1 - HH = 1 - \Sigma p^2_i$$

F also varies from 0 to 1. Extreme concentration corresponds to zero fractionalization and vice versa.

Mayer's A is based on the number of parties represented plus the relative share of the largest party. Mayer defines the index as

$$A = (S/L)/P$$

where A is the aggregation index, S is the mean number of seats that the largest party in any given legislative session has for the period in question, L is the mean number of seats in the lower house of the legislature for the period, and P is the mean number of parties holding seats in that house averaged for the period in question (1980 B, 338-339).

In most situations, the two indices can be expected to display a clear negative correlation. In a situation where there is one relatively large party and a great number of clearly smaller parties they produce, however, significantly different results, which is why they can be seen as alternative or complementary measures of party system fragmentation (Mayer 1980 A, 518). While the F is expected to covary positively with instability and breakdown, the A is expected to display a negative correlation.

As for the polarization score, the measure employed simply denotes the total percentage of seats held by communist, socialist, conservative and right wing extremist parties[1] (cf. Myklebust and Ugelvik Larsen 1980, 636).

All values of variables referred to below are averages for the individual countries. If nothing else is indicated, analyses are based on arithmetic means for the entire period (for the 'survivors' basically 1920-39; for the five cases of 'breakdown', up until the last parliament and cabinet before the authoritarian takeover). Except for Italy, the data were also divided into two sub-periods (roughly 'the 1920s' and the '1930s').

Standard statistical techniques were employed to describe the degree of association between the various factors. First, the two basic groups of countries, 'survival' and 'breakdown' were scrutinized in the light of the explanatory variables. After that, cabinet instability was examined in a similar way. For the former tests, cross-tabulation techniques and tests of significance were used. For cross-tabulation, the explanatory variables were dichotomized ('high' and 'low') on the basis of median values for the entire sample. For tests of cabinet instability, Pearson correlation coefficients appear in the text. Here, the limited number of cases restricts the use of this statistical technique. It was, however, checked against cross-tabulation techniques less sensitive to a small N; the results were similar. Nevertheless, given the small number of cases the statistical tests should be seen as fairly 'soft' descriptive instruments.

Findings: bivariate relationships

For those who expected straightforward connections between party systemic characteristics, cabinet stability and the survival/breakdown of democracy, Tables 2 and 3 may be somewhat of a disappointment:

---

[1]. This is, of course, a far from unproblematic measure. The alternative would have been to use only communist and right wing extremist strength as an indicator. This would, however, have overlooked the fact that the ideological and strategic positions of the noncommunist Left varied a great deal. Had the alternative measure been selected, countries like Austria would have scored low on polarization; this seems clearly counter-intuitive. Nevertheless, it should be stressed that our measure of polarization is an indicator of the weakness of the Center rather than of extremism on the Left and Right wings. It should also be noted that the 'communist factor' is included in our analysis since the fractionalization of the Left is one of the variables studied systematically.

Table 2. The breakdown and survival of democracy in interwar Europe: average values of explanatory factors for two groups of countries

Variable	'Survival' (min/max)	'Breakdown' (min/max)
1. Number of parties in parliament	8.1 (5.1/15.5)	12.6 (3.8/25.0)
1. Period I	7.9 (5.5/16.0)	13.0 (3.7/25.0)
1. Period II	8.3 (4.5/15.0)	12.8 (4.0/25.0)
2. Fraction- alization of parliament	0.74 (0.56/0.90)	0.78 (0.62/0.90)
2. Period I	0.76 (0.60/0.90)	0.81 (0.62/0.88)
2. Period II	0.73 (0.51/0.90)	0.79 (0.64/0.92)
3. Party ag- gregation of parliament	5.4 (1.2/9.3)	4.4 (1.1/12.3)
3. Period I	5.1 (1.3/8.6)	4.7 (1.3/12.8)
3. Period II	5.5 (1.1/10.5)	4.4 (0.9/10.9)
4. Polar- ization of parliament	66.4 (43.7/86.3)	65.1 (43.3/100)
4. Period I	65.4 (47.7/82.5)	67.2 (46.5/100)
4. Period II	67.3 (42.1/87.7)	70.6 (40.0/100)
5. Fraction- alization of nonsocialist parties	0.64 (0.37/0.86)	0.69 (0.38/0.93)
5. Period I	0.65 (0.42/0.86)	0.73 (0.35/0.94)
5. Period II	0.64 (0.31/0.87)	0.69 (0.45/0.93)
6. Fraction- alization of socialist p.	0.20 (0.0/0.72)	0.29 (0.0/0.47)
6. Period I	0.22 (0.0/0.72)	0.32 (0.0/0.51)
6. Period II	0.20 (0.0/0.73)	0.32 (0.0/0.51)
7. Cabinet	734 (182/2400)	245 (157/302)

duration (A)

7. Period I	696 (212/2380)		275 (248/303)
7. Period II	868 (158/2410)		250 (229/302)

8. Cabinet duration (B)	1059 (222/3601)		329 (275/414)
8. Period I	736 (280/2380)		388 (303/531)
8. Period II	1288 (174/2411)		282 (231/319)

Legend: For each independent variable, the first figure is based on the average for the entire period, the second for roughly 1920-30, and the third for the period from about 1930 on. Italy is included only in the averages for the entire period
Variables 7 and 8 do not include Switzerland

Table 3. The correlates of the breakdown/survival of democracy in interwar Europe

Variable	F (sig.)	T (sig.)	Chi sq. (sig.)	Phi	N
1. Number of parties in parliament	0.22	0.27	0.67	0.24	16
1. Period I	0.28	0.34	0.31	0.26	15
1. Period II	0.36	0.41	0.18	0.34	15
2. Fraction- alization of parliament	0.65	0.49	0.60	0.14	16
2. Period I	0.49	0.52	0.18	0.34	15
2. Period II	0.44	0.47	0.31	0.26	15
3.Party ag- gregation of parliament	0.66	0.68	0.10	0.41	16
3. Period I	0.86	0.88	0.18	0.34	15
3. Period II	0.65	0.67	0.18	0.34	15
4. Polar- ization of parliament	0.90	0.90	0.60	0.14	16
4. Period I	0.88	0.89	0.31	0.26	15
4. Period II	0.81	0.82	0.87	0.04	15

5. Fractionalization of nonsocialist parties	0.66	0.67	0.60	0.14	16
5. Period I	0.61	0.64	0.18	0.34	15
5. Period II	0.61	0.63	0.31	0.26	15
6. Fractionalization of socialist p.	0.48	0.48	0.62	0.22	16
6. Period I	0.52	0.52	0.18	0.34	15
6. Period II	0.40	0.41	0.18	0.34	15
7. Cabinet duration (A)	0.03[*]	0.04[*]	0.01[*]	0.66[*]	15
7. Period I	0.06	0.06	0.02[*]	0.63[*]	14
7. Period II	0.02[*]	0.02[*]	0.02[*]	0.63[*]	14
8. Cabinet duration (B)	0.04[*]	0.05[*]	0.01[*]	0.66[*]	15
8. Period I	0.10	0.11	0.24	0.32	14
8. Period II	0.02[*]	0.02[*]	0.24	0.32	14

*) significant values
Cabinet duration A = all cabinets
Cabinet duration B = only cabinets entailing a change of Prime Minister counted as 'new cabinets'.

Looking at the *average values* for the explanatory factors, the two groups of countries would seem to conform to the basic theoretical expectations described above. On the whole, the successful democracies had less fragmented party systems (in terms of number of parties, fractionalization and aggregation) than those countries where democracy went under. As for polarization, this average difference is less clear. By contrast, cabinet stability was clearly higher in the successful democracies than in our cases of 'breakdown'.

Save for the last factor, however, the picture is complicated by the *spread* of variable values within the two groups. Both groups include concentrated as well as fragmented party systems. By the same token, cases of both high and low polarization are to be found in both groups. Most 'survivors' display low or moderate degrees of fragmentation, but the Netherlands, Switzerland and especially Czechoslovakia are highly fragmented. The degree of polarization in the Low Countries and Great Britain is almost twice as high as in Ireland; other cases form an even spread between these extremes.

As for the five cases of 'breakdown', Austria clearly is the 'deviant case'. The other countries have high levels of fragmentation (Latvia being hyperfractionalized) and low or moderate degrees of polarization (save for Germany in the 1930s). Austria, by contrast, has the most concentrated party system in entire Europe, and it is totally polarized in the sense that there is no centrist party between the socialists and their clearly conservative rivals.

What separates the 'survivors' from the cases of breakdown is their higher degree of cabinet stability. However, even here the variance among the survivors is considerable. Moreover, there is one clear exception to this pattern: France. It has consistently the lowest degree of cabinet stability of *all* countries included in the study. Despite this, the five cases of 'breakdown' are conspicious by their uniformly low levels of cabinet stability.

As a consequence of this variance within the two groups, the variables describing party system characteristics consistently fail to display significant degrees of association with the fate of democracy in interwar Europe. Most of the values are in fact very low. Moreover, the variation between the two sub-periods also proves to be low, thus indicating that there were few significant changes in the general rank-ordering of the countries on these dimensions.

By contrast, we can again note the reasonably clear (but not very surprising) relationship between cabinet instability and the fate of democracy in interwar Europe. All those countries where democracy broke down had a short average cabinet duration, wheras most countries in the 'survival' group had relatively stable cabinets. Evidently, cabinet instability was a necessary, although not a sufficient, condition for the breakdown of democracy in interwar Europe.

What, then, is the relationship between party systemic factors and cabinet duration? Table 4 sheds some light on this question.

Table 4. The correlates of cabinet duration in interwar Europe. Pearson correlation coefficients.

	All cabinets		'New cabinets'	
Variable	*r*	*sig.*	*r*	*sig.*

1. Number of parties in parliament	-0.31	0.26	-0.28	0.31
1. Period I	-0.22	0.45	-0.26	0.36
1. Period II	-0.31	0.29	-0.18	0.53
2. Fractional- ization of parl.	-0.33	0.23	-0.27	0.33
2. Period I	-0.04	0.89	-0.08	0.78
2. Period II	-0.39	0.17	-0.25	0.39
3. Party aggreg. of parliament	0.41	0.12	0.36	0.19
3. Period I	0.16	0.59	0.22	0.44
3. Period II	0.43	0.12	0.20	0.48
4. Polarization of parliament	-0.32	0.25	-0.28	0.32
4. Period I	-0.29	0.32	-0.22	0.44
4. Period II	-0.40	0.16	-0.22	0.45
5. Fractional- ization of non- socialist parties	-0.09	0.76	-0.06	0.84
5. Period I	-0.06	0.98	-0.06	0.82
5. Period II	-0.03	0.90	0.04	0.87
6. Fractional- ization of socialist p.	-0.45	0.09	-0.42	0.12
6. Period I	-0.43	0.12	-0.46	0.09
6. Period II	-0.49	0.08	-0.37	0.20

'New cabinets' = only cabinets entailing a change of Prime Minister counted as separate cabinets
N = for the entire period, 15, for sub-periods, 14

Switzerland was omitted from the analyses concerning cabinets; the Swiss system with fixed term collegiate Federal Councils makes the question of cabinet duration rather meaningless. As for the countries included, the picture is reasonably clear. Not one correlation is, strictly speaking, statistically significant; at the same time, the general *direction* of the correlations matches our expectations. In other words, there is a slight tendency in the data indicating that countries with short-lived cabinets had more fragmented and polarized party systems than stable countries. Of the independent variables, party aggregation and the fragmentation of the left wing approach significant values. Nevertheless, in purely statistical terms party systemic variables fail to provide a satisfactory explanation of cabinet duration.

Several authors, Sani and Sartori in particular, stress the role of *polarization* as a threat to the stability of democracy. In particular, when polarization is combined with high fragmentation such negative effects are expected to appear. In our sample, however, only three countries (Germany, Holland and France) displayed high values on both dimensions. Obviously, this explanation is far from sufficient to account for either the fate of interwar European democracy or for the degree of cabinet stability. In fact, polarization in terms of the structure of party systems covaried negatively (r=-0.45) with the fractionalization of parliaments. Consequently, fractionalization often leads to a *lower* degree of polarization since many of the 'fractions' are centrist or ethnic parties rather than left or right wing parties. As for polarization as such, tables 2 and 3 above show that it its independent explanatory power is very low. Those countries which displayed high levels of party system polarization (Sweden, Belgium, United Kingdom, Germany, France, Austria and the Netherlands) represented as heterogeneous a group of countries as one might possibly picture in interwar Europe.

By the same token, there were only two cases (Switzerland and Norway) that matched my earlier proposition about a *cohesive left in conjunction with a fractionalized nonsocialist wing*. Again, the problem with this proposition was that the fractionalization of the socialist and nonsocialist wings was positively interrelated (r=0.50). Where fragmentation was high, it usually concerned both wings; where the Left was cohesive, the nonsocialist wing was usually not fragmented above the median value for the entire sample.

Whether in fact there was a significant interplay between party systemic factors and cabinet instability in the process toward this outcome can not, however, be determined through bivariate statistical correlations only. Therefore, the remainder of our aggregate-level analysis will direct attention to the more complex interplay between the three main dimensions.

Three main dimensions: combinations

The original 'theory' about the effects of party system fragmentation discussed at the outset of this study views fragmentation, cabinet instability and the breakdown of democracy as part and parcel of the same syndrome. The one leads to the other; fragmentation breeds instability, instability paves the way for an authoritarian takeover.

The data presented above shows that this proposition is not upheld when it is translated into operationalized variables and relations between such variables. There is, to be sure, a statistical link between cabinet duration and the ultimate fate of democracy; party system characteristics fail, however, to explain why some democracies went under while the majority survived. Moreover, their explanatory power proved limited also as concerns variations in cabinet duration.

In this section, this 'variable-centered' approach is complemented with a 'case-centered' view. The idea is that even if there is no general correlation between specific variables in the data at large, it is not impossible that certain *combinations* of variables may help understand the peculiarities of *individual cases.*

A bird's eye view

We shall start by returning to our original matrix (Table 1) to see how the various cases rank on the three basic dimensions. 'High' and 'low' values of party system fragmentation are determined on the basis of median values of fractionalization and party aggregation of parliament. For cabinet instability, average cabinet duration (all cabinets) was used in the same way.

Table 5. Party system fragmentation, cabinet instability and the fate of democracy in sixteen countries in interwar Europe.

Cabinet instability

| *Low* | *High* |

		Breakdown?			
		No	*Yes*	*No*	*Yes*
	Low	Denmark		(Finland)	Austria
		Norway		(Belgium)	
Frag-		Sweden			
ment-		UK			
ation		Ireland			
	High	Netherlands		France	Estonia
		Czechoslovakia			Germany
		Switzerland			Latvia
					(Italy)

Finland, Belgium and Italy constitute borderline cases. The Finnish value for the fractionalization of parliament was almost exactly the median value for the entire group; as its party aggregation was slightly above the median value, Finland was ascribed to the 'low fragmentation' category. For Italy it was the other way around; here, however, party aggregation remained more clearly below the median. Cabinet duration in Belgium was insignificantly below the median for the entire group. Finally, the Swiss cabinet practice naturally makes it somewhat inaccurate to speak of 'high or low cabinet duration' in this case. The argument for placing Switzerland in this category would be that the Swiss *system* of fixed-term Federal Councils remained stable throughout the period.

Even given these caveats, however, this table complements the picture provided by the statistical analysis above. What stands out as 'no or low association' when looking at bivariate relations across cases, appears as a much more intriguing picture when individual countries are at the center of the attention. Nine out of sixteen cases turn out to belong to 'paradigmatic types', i.e., display either 'low fragmentation, low instability and no breakdown' or 'high fragmentation, high instability and breakdown'. The five countries in the first type are all unitary states situated in Northwestern Europe; they are all characterized by high degrees of cultural and ethnic homogeneity. The fact that such countries were among the 'survivors' from the crisis of European democracy is of course a well-known fact. It is, however, noteworthy that these same states also ranked lowest on party system fragmentation and cabinet instability.

As for Estonia, Germany, Latvia and Italy it is more difficult to find self-evident common denominators apart from the three dimensions comprised by the model. Save for the two Baltic countries of Estonia and Latvia, they vary widely in size, geographic location, ethnic and religious composition etc.

By contrast, the three countries which had high levels of party system fragmentation without high cabinet instability and ensuing breakdown of democracy seem to share some important common characteristics. Holland, Czechoslovakia and Switzerland are all *segmented* societies, and the fragmentation of their party systems is largely a reflection of this segmentation. At the same time, this segmentation apparently did not hamper political stability or the position of democracy.

These kinds of reflections must, however, be preliminary at this stage not the least because the remaining four cases seem quite puzzling in the light of the model. At this time, we must content ourselves with preliminarily summarizing our findings thus far as follows:

1 The survival or breakdown of democracy does not appear to be explicable in terms of bivariate statistical relationships between party system characteristics and the ultimate fate of democracy.

2 By contrast, cabinet duration seems to offer a statistically significant explanation of the breakdown or survival of democracy; cabinet instability in these terms appears to be a necessary but not a sufficient condition for the breakdown of democracy.

3 The fragmentation of the party system is to some extent related to cabinet instability; these relationships are, however, not statistically significant.

4 'Polarized fragmentation' and the relative fragmentation of the socialist and nonsocialist wings do not constitute adequate explanations of either the breakdown of democracy or the degree of cabinet instability.

5 When the median values of the main explanatory dimensions (fragmentation and instability) are combined, roughly half of the cases comply with the suppositions of the original theory.

In his critique of the post-WWII 'two-party theory' Arend Lijphart notes that

> The evidence does show that multipartism is associated with relatively short-lived cabinets, but its is also a mistake to regard such cabinet 'instability' as an indicator of fundamental regime instability (1984, 111).

In much the same vein Lawrence Mayer points to the fact that

> These two conceptualizations of political stability [constitutional and cabinet stability] are not clearly distinguished in the literature; yet, there is a more or less explicit suggestion in the literature that a breakdown in the latter will ultimately cause a breakdown in the former. This idea is never put in quantified terms with clearly specified threshold levels and, hence, is not rigorously falsifiable in the form of more than x amount of cabinet instability will result in y amount of constitutional instability in z circumstances. One cannot even say at what point cabinet instability will result in any unspecified but significant increase in the level of constitutional instability. The variable of constitutional instability inherently involves such a small N that statistical techniques are inappropriate for manipulating such data (1989, 152).

The problem of the limited N pointed out by Mayer is inescapable and certainly acute in the present study. Moreover, our analysis can hardly be credited with having specified critical 'threshold values' for cabinet instability. Yet if anything, our data go to reverse Lijphart's assertion (which was based on a review of research on post-WWII democracies). It is clear from our tests pertaining to the interwar period that party system fragmentation has limited (although not entirely negligible) explanatory power for cabinet duration; by contrast, short cabinet duration seems to be significantly related to the 'ultimate regime instability', i.e., the breakdown of democracy. Although clearly insufficient as an overall explanation, the original theory at least seems to point in the right direction as concerns the general dynamics of European democracy in the interwar period.

Empirical analysis II: country by country

This section shifts the attention from the general levels of fragmentation and stability to *relative changes* within individual countries. As was pointed out above, part of the previous research has been involved in the search of the determinants of government and constitutional stability at the level of the individual nation.

The basic hypothesis could be stated as follows:
Marked increases in party system fragmentation are negatively related to cabinet stability; the breakdown of democracy is expected to be preceded by such marked changes in fragmentation and the survivability of cabinets.

A variant of this hypothesis might be one that presupposes the existence of *critical thresholds*: it was not change as such but change above a certain level of fragmentation that affected the survivability of cabinets and the democratic system itself.

The following analysis seeks to pinpoint any clear changes in the party system variables for each country separately. These are then related to possible subsequent changes in cabinet and constitutional stability.

The starting point is, consequently, the structure of each individual parliament. This structure (in terms of party composition) may of course change as a consequence of each election. For each country, we therefore start by presenting values of party system variables for each parliamentary period. After that, average values of cabinet stability are shown for corresponding periods. In most cases, it is possible to assign each cabinet to a given parliamentary period; cabinets resign either a short period before an election or shortly after it. Several times, however, cabinets and parliaments were 'out of step' with each other. In such cases, a somewhat different periodization was necessary. These choices are at all times evident from the footnotes attached to each table.

The following abbreviations apply to all tables:

N = number of parties in parliament

F = Rae's index of fractionalization

A = Mayer's index of party aggregation

P = polarization of parliament (the combined shares of Left and Right)

FB = fractionalization of nonsocialist parties (Rae)

FS = fractionalization of socialist parties (Rae)

CabA = average cabinet duration in days in a given period

CabB = average cabinet duration when only cabinets entailing a change of Prime Minister are counted as new cabinets (NB: when no value is given for a period, there was only one Prime Minister during this period, and he was the same person as the last Prime Minister of the previous period)

The order of presentation is the same as in the historical narratives in Chapter II.

Italy

	1919	1921
N	9	12
F	0.72	0.74
A	3.9	3.8
P	50.6	52.7
FB	0.59	0.61
FS	0.08	0.22
	1919-21[a]	1921-22

CabA	171	139
CabB	342	208

a) Including Giolitti's cabinet which resigned on June 27, 1921 (election June 15).

Despite the increased number of parties in the *Camera dei Deputati*, the fragmentation of the Italian parliament increased only marginally and remained on a moderate overall level. Similarly, the entry of the fascists into the parliament was accompanied by stronger shares for the liberals, which is why the fractionalization of the nonsocialist camp increased only marginally. By some contrast, the split between the socialists and the communists had a clearer effect on the fractionalization of the Left. Cabinet duration fell from short to very short during the period.

All in all, the changes preceding the fascist takeover in Italy point in the right direction from thge point of view of the fragmentation thesis. All the same, they can hardly be described as particularly dramatic; clearly, the fragmentation of Italian politics remained on the same *general level* throughout the period.

Germany

	1920	1924	1924	1928	1930	1932	1932
N	10	13	11	15	15	14	13
F	0.85	0.87	0.87	0.84	0.88	0.77	0.80
A	2.2	1.8	2.4	2.1	1.7	2.7	2.6
P	61.4	64.6	63.3	64.8	72.8	84.2	84.6
FB	0.78	0.82	0.82	0.83	0.84	0.62	0.65
FS	0.51	0.47	0.38	0.38	0.46	0.58	0.50

	1920-24[a]	1924[b]	1924-28[c]	1928-32[d]	1932-33[e]
CabA	189	201	289	456	99
CabB	252		577	685	99

a)incl. W. Marx res. May 26, 1924 (election May 4)
b)only W. Marx res. Dec., 15, 1924 (election Dec. 7)
c)incl. W.Marx res. June 12, 1928 (election June 20)
d)incl. Brüning res. May 20, 1932 (election July 31)
e)incl. von Schleicher res. Jan. 28, 1933

The *Reichstag* was one of the most fragmented parliaments in Europe throughout the interwar period. There was, however, no *increase* of fragmentation over time. In fact, the German parliament became somewhat less fragmented in the years immediately before the nazi takeover. Similarly, due to the rise to prominence of the National Socialists, the degree of fragmentation of the nonsocialist camp diminished in the early 1930s, while the fractionalization of the Left parties continued at roughly the same level as previously. The most marked change concerns polarization, which increased considerably because of the rise of the nazis, the concomitant collapse of the middle parties, and the simultaneous strengthening of the communists.

Cabinet stability was rather low in the first five years; however, throughout the 1920s there was marked element of personal continuity in German cabinet politics. Wilhelm Marx headed 4 different cabinets, Josef Wirth, Gustav Stresemann, Hans Luther and Hermann Müller two each. From the mid-1920s up until the Great Depression, there was a trend toward increased cabinet durability. The remaining cabinets before *Machtergreifung* were short-lived.

By way of conclusion, therefore, there was no increase in fragmentation connected to the final political instability in the early 1930s. By contrast, the increase in parliamentary polarization matches the time-sequence of the German democratic breakdown quite well.

Austria

	1920	1923	1927	1930
N	5	5	4	5

F	0.66	0.60	0.59	0.64
A	11.6	12.1	14.7	10.9
P	100	100	100	100
FB	0.39	0.31	0.35	0.45
FS	0	0	0	0

	1920-23[a]	1923-27[b]	1927-30[c]	1930-33[d]
CabA	225	315	306	237
CabB	376	630	407	316

a)incl. Seipel res. Nov. 19, 1923 (election Oct. 21)
b)incl. Seipel res. May 19, 1927 (election April 24)
c)incl. Vaugoin res. Nov. 29, 1930 (election Nov. 9)
d)incl. Dollfuss res. sept. 21, 1933

The Austrian party system remains quite stable throughout the period preceding the breakdown of democracy. The degree of fragmentation is low and the degree of polarization is high. The 1927 election in particular creates a strongly concentrated party constellation in the *Nationalrat*. Fragmentation increases somewhat toward the end of the period being roughly on the same level as at the beginning. Cabinet duration is short especially at the beginning and the end of the period, but a relatively high degree of personal continuity can be noted. If the focus is on the period 1927-33 one might say that increased fragmentation is followed by greater cabinet instability and a subsequent breakdown of democracy. It would, nevertheless, be an exaggeration to characterize the change in relative fragmentation as dramatic.

Estonia

	1920	1923	1926	1929	1932
N	10	14	10	10	6
F	0.86	0.89	0.84	0.84	0.72

A	2.2	2.3	2.4	2.5	4.2
P	53.0	63.0	60.0	62.0	not relevant[a]
FB	0.77	0.84	0.80	0.80	0.57
FS	0.60	0.61	0.32	0.31	0.31

	1920-23	1923-26	1926-29	1929-32	1932-33
CabA 336		270	265	272	150
CabB 336		270	529	272	150

a) the main right-wing and centrist parties merged into a catch-all United Peasant Party (cf. Mägi 1967, 180-182).
NB: Estonian cabinets always resigned subsequent to an election; elections were held in May except in 1920 (when it was held in November).

The Estonian case is highly discomforting from the point of view of the fragmentation thesis. To be sure, the Estonian party system remained strongly fragmented through most of the democractic period. Similarly, cabinet duration was short and the degree of personal continuity fairly limited. However, just prior to the collapse of Estonian democracy the party system became considerably *less* fragmented than before. This was largely due to the consolidation of the nonsocialist parties leading to a reduction in their number before the 1932 election. At the same time, there had been a gradual decrease in the fragmentation of the Left, although the left wing still remained fragmented clearly above the general European level. For all practical purposes, the Estonian case runs *counter* to the hypothesis about the importance of relative changes in party system fragmentation. Decreased fragmentation was followed by increased cabinet instability and ultimately by the breakdown of democracy itself.

Latvia

1922 1925 1928 1931

N	22	28	27	23
F	0.88	0.87	0.91	0.92
A	1.4	1.1	0.9	0.9
P	47.0	46.0	44.0	36.0
FB	0.93	0.95	0.93	0.92
FS	0.35	0.29	0.49	0.43

	1922-25[a]	1925-28[b]	1928-31[c]	1931-34
CabA	348	269	340	277
CabB	348	269	340	277

a) Incl. Celmins res. Dec. 25, 1925 (election Nov.)
b) Incl. Jurasesvkis res. Nov. 13, 1928 (election Oct.)
c) Incl. Ulmanis res. Nov. 4, 1931 (election Oct. 1931)

Latvia remained a hyperfractionalized system throughout the period. The fact that there were five parties less in the *saeima* in 1931 than in 1925 did not decrease the level of fragmentation of the party system. This was mainly due to the fact that there was a simultaneous increase in fractionalization on the Left. At the same time, cabinet duration remained short throughout the period. All in all, the Latvian picture is one of permanent fragmentation and cabinet instability rather than any marked change.

England

	1918	1922	1923	1924	1929	1931	1935
N	8	7	5	6	5	9	9
F	0.65	0.62	0.65	0.47	0.59	0.40	0.54
A	6.8	8.0	8.4	11.2	8.5	8.5	7.0
P	62.8	79.2	73.0	92.2	88.9	85.3	88.9
FB	0.60	0.45	0.43	0.19	0.34	0.31	0.28
FS	0	0.01	0	0.01	0	0.22	0.06

	1918-22[a]	1922-23[b]	1923-24[c]	1924-29[d]	1929-31[e]
CabA	1042	453	253	1699	440
CabB		453	253	1699	880

	1931-35[f]	1935-40[g]
CabA	1341	899
CabB		899

a) only Lloyd Geoge res. Oct. 19, 1922 (election Nov. 15)
b) only Bonar Law res. Jan. 22, 1924 (election Dec. 6, 1923)
c) only MacDonald res. Nov. 4, 1924 (election Oct. 29)
d) only Baldwin res. June 4, 1929 (election May 30)
e) incl. MacDonald res. Nov. 5, 1931 (election Oct. 27)
f) only MacDonald res. June 7, 1935 (election Nov. 14)
g) incl. Chamberlain res. May 10, 1940

The English party system was characterized by low degrees of fragmentation throughout the period. With the temporary exception of 1923-1924, cabinet stability was moderate to high. There were, however, rather notable changes on some points. The degree of fragmentation varied to some extent, and especially the consolidation of the nonsocialist side is rather clear. Interestingly enough, both those periods (1924-29 and 1931-35) which displayed the highest cabinet stability were characterized by the lowest values of fractionalization. By the same token, the least stable period (1923-24) displayed a relatively high degree of fractionalization (but no corresponding low figure for party aggregation). It should however, be noted that the highest overall fragmentation in 1918-22 coincided with a relatively long cabinet duration.

All in all, nevertheless, the changes in the English party system seem largely compatible with the fragmentation thesis.

Ireland

	1923	1927	1927	1932	1933	1937	1938
N	5	7	7	5	5	4	4
F	0.72	0.79	0.68	0.63	0.64	0.62	0.58
A	8.2	4.4	6.8	9.4	10.1	12.5	13.9
P	50.3	45.1	49.0	41.8	36.6	44.2	39.1
FB	0.68	0.75	0.62	0.60	0.60	0.55	0.52
FS	0	0	0	0	0	0	0

	1923-32[a]	1932-44[b]
CabA 1527	4147	
CabB 3057	4147	

a) incl. Cosgrave res. March 9, 1932 (election Febr. 16)
b) only de Valera

The Irish case is special, even extreme in a certain sense. To be sure, through most of the 1920s the Irish party system is a moderately fragmentated one and thus much in line with the general European situation. The degree of fragmentation decreased gradually, however, and at the end of the 1930s Ireland had one of the most concentrated party systems of all European democracies. In contrast to all other cases, this process of defractionalization was accompanied by decreasing polarization; in fact, Ireland had one of the least polarized party systems at the end of the period. The fact that even the fractionalization of the nonsocialist wing decreased simultaneously adds still another special feature to the Irish case.

It is concerning cabinets, however, that Ireland really seems *sui generis* in a European comparison. From the first elections after the establishment of the Irish Free State up until 1948, Ireland only had two different Prime Ministers, William Cosgrave and Eamonn de Valera. If the reshuffle of Cosgrave's cabinet in 1930 is disregarded, one may also say that there were only two different cabinets in the period until the second world war. Irish cabinet stability, therefore, is unparalleled throughout the rest of Europe. If one wishes to press our findings one might argue that the decreasing fragmentation of the party system was accompanied by ever higher cabinet stability in Ireland. Nevertheless, the main impression of Irish cabinet duration is one of massive continuity rather than change.

France

	1919	1924	1928	1932	1936
N	8	6	9	10	5
F	0.80	0.75	0.82	0.84	0.76
A	3.6	5.9	3.4	2.7	7.3
P	78.6	90.7	78.2	76.0	not relevant[a]
FB	0.68	0.43	0.64	0.79	0
FS	0.58	0.55	0.64	0.62	0.72

	1919-24[b]	1924-28[c]	1928-32[d]	1932-36[e]	1936-40
CabA	310	175	140	120	275
CabB	388	263	181	120	343

a) nonsocialists formed a National Front before the 1936 election
b) incl. Poincaré res. June 1, 1924 (election May 11)
c) incl. Poincaré res. Nov. 6, 1928 (election April 22)
d) incl. Tardieu res. May 10, 1932 (election May 1)
e) incl. Sarraut res. June 4, 1936 (election April 26)

Any attempt to describe the French parliamentary party system in exact terms will remain controversial. In fact, there are those who have questioned the existence of parties in France in general, at least on the nonsocialist side: 'The parties of the Right and Center (including the Radicals) constituted "parties of notables", which means that, basically, they were not parties at all' (Hermens 1958, 268). The broad *tendances* typical of French politics were a far cry from disciplined parliamentary party groups. Our decision to follow Mackie and Rose (Table 7.3c) even as concerns the 1936 election is certainly open to criticism, as it leads to quite a clear change in the total picture: the National

Front, the electoral alliance comprising the Independent radicals, Left Radicals, Republican Union as well as the Conservatives and Independents was certainly not a party merger in any normal sense of the term. On the other hand, since the definition of the parties constituting the front was equally problematic, it is in accordance with the logic of our analysis to follow Mackie and Rose on this point. Caution is nevertheless in order when interpreting the figures for 1936.

Party system fragmentation ranged from moderate to high in France. Cabinet stability was low throughout the period, being extremely low in the ten-year period from the mid 1920s to the mid-1930s. The relative increase in cabinet stability in the second half of the 1930s would seem to go hand in hand with a decreased parliamentary fragmentation. In view of what was said above about the French party system, this finding mus, however, be interpreted with a considerable amount of caution.

Belgium

	1919	1921	1925	1929	1932	1936	1939
N	7	6	6	6	5	7	7
F	0.68	0.67	0.64	0.70	0.65	0.77	0.73
A	5.6	6.8	7.0	6.3	8.4	5.0	5.2
P	80.1	80.0	86.1	81.8	87.1	87.6	82.7
FB	0.51	0.52	0.46	0.56	0.45	0.67	0.59
FS	0	0	0.05	0.03	0.08	0.21	0.22

	1919-21[a]	1921-25[b]	1925-29[c]	1929-32[d]
CabA	338	423	403	330
CabB	338	845	538	440

	1932-36[e]	1936-39[f]
CabA	371	248

CabB 557   331

a) incl. Carton de Wiart res. Nov. 19, 1921 (election Nov. 20)
b) incl. Theunis res. April 5, 1925 (election May 5)
c) incl. Jaspar res. Nov. 26, 1929 (election May 26, 1929)
d) incl. de Broqueville res. Dec. 13, 1932 (election Nov. 27)
e) incl. van Zeeland res. May 26, 1936 (election May 24)
f) incl. Pierlot res. April 12, 1939 (election April 2)

The Belgian party system was moderately fragmented. Fragmentation was highest during the second half of the 1930s when also the communists gained representation, thus fractionalizing the Left to a certain degree. The very beginning of the interwar period was also characterized by somewhat higher fragmentation than the years in between, particularly the 1932-36 period.

Cabinet duration was low to moderate with an element of personal continuity clearly visible through most of the period. The shortest average cabinet duration occurs after the 1936 election, thus coinciding with the peak of party system fragmentation. Interestingly enough, the beginning of the period displays a similar pattern, and so does the 1929-32 period as well. Certainly, none of the changes is particularly marked, but still this pattern would seem to corroborate the basic hypothesis about the importance of relative changes in party system fragmentation.

The Netherlands

	1922	1925	1929	1933	1937
N	10	11	11	14	10
F	0.81	0.81	0.82	0.84	0.82
A	3.2	2.7	2.7	2.0	3.1
P	82.0	82.0	83.0	81.0	88.0
FB	0.75	0.77	0.77	0.77	0.76
FS	0.16	0.08	0.14	0.32	0.21

	1922-25[a]	1925-29[b]	1929-33[c]	1933-37[d]	1937-39[e]
CabA	1066	660	1361	731	371
CabB	1066	660	1361	1461	742

a) only de Beerenbrouck res. Aug. 1, 1925 (election July 1)
b) incl. de Geer res. July 3, 1929 (election July 3)
c) only de Beerenbrouck res. April 26, 1933 (election April 26)
d) incl. Colijn res. May 27, 1937 (election May 26)
e) incl. Colijn res. July 27, 1939

The Dutch party system was highly fragmented throughout the period, and the changes from election to election were small. The disappearance of four minor parties from the *Tweede Kamer* as a result of the 1937 election had but a minor impact on our other measures of fragmentation. Similarly, although there were variations in cabinet stability, it remained moderate to high throughout the period. There was a strong element of personal continuity in Dutch cabinet politics. Whatever the cause of the variation, it does not seem plausible to relate it to our data on the relative changes in party system fragmentation.

Switzerland

	1919	1922	1925	1928	1931	1935	1939
N	7	8	9	9	9	12	10
F	0.77	0.78	0.79	0.78	0.76	0.80	0.82
A	3.5	3.8	3.8	3.3	3.1	2.2	2.5
P	48.1	49.0	51.0	52.5	54.0	54.0	52.4
FB	0.72	0.72	0.71	0.69	0.71	0.75	0.75
FS	0	0.05	0.11	0.08	0.08	0.08	0.15

Switzerland is a special case which could well be omitted from this examination, since the concept of cabinet duration is not relevant in the Swiss case at all. Nevertheless, even if it were relevant (and even if there had been a breakdown of democracy in Switzerland), it is difficult to see how this could be related to *changes* in the Swiss party system. Throughout the period, the Swiss party system was relatively fragmented with a low degree of polarization. Even if some increase in fragmentation can be discerned at the end of the period, the overall picture is one of almost complete continuity.

Czechoslovakia

	1920	1925	1929	1935
N	17	15	16	14
F	0.89	0.91	0.93	0.85
A	1.5	1.0	1.0	1.1
P	58.4	57.3	57.3	54.3
FB	0.85	0.87	0.87	0.86
FS	0.65	0.79	0.74	0.71

	1920-25[a]	1925-29[b]	1929-35[c]	1935-38
CabA	629	378	674	224
CabB	629	503	1010	672

a) incl. Svehla res. Nov. 16, 1925 (election Nov. 15)
b) incl. Udrzal res. Oct. 28, 1929 (election Oct. 27)
c) incl. Malypetr res. May 29, 1935 (election May 19)

Czechoslovakia remained hyperfractionalized throughout the interwar period. The variations were small, especially when the combined values of the variables describinng fragmentation are considered. Polarization remained low during the entire period. Cabinet duration varied somewhat, being moderate most of the time; a fairly high personal continuity can be noted. The most notable change concerns the second half of the 1930s. However, if anything this change is accompanied by a slight *decrease* in party system fragmentation.

In sum, the question of relative changes in party system fragmentation is not particularly relevant in the Czechoslovak context.

Denmark

	1920	1920	1920	1924	1926	1929	1932	1934	1939
N	5	5	6	5	6	6	7	8	9
F	0.74	0.73	0.73	0.71	0.72	0.71	0.71	0.71	0.73
A	6.9	7.3	5.7	7.4	6.0	6.9	6.0	5.7	4.8
P	50.3	48.9	50.7	56.1	56.1	57.4	60.1	63.5	60.8
FB	0.65	0.62	0.64	0.63	0.64	0.66	0.67	0.73	0.74
FS	0	0	0	0	0	0	0.07	0.06	0.09

	1920-24[a]	1924-26[b]	1926-29[c]	1929-35[d]	1935-40
CabA	367	953	906	1985	1892
CabB	489	953	906	1985	

a) incl. Neergaard res. April 22, 1924 (election April 11)
b) only Stauning res. Dec. 2, 1926 (election Dec. 2)
c) only Madsen-Mygdal res. April 25, 1929 (election April 24)
d) only Stauning res. Nov. 4, 1935 (election Oct. 22)

A constitutional crisis pertaining to the border region between Germany and Denmark gave rise to several consecutive elections in Denmark in 1920. These did not, however, alter the level of fragmentation or polarization of the Danish parliament. In fact, the Danish picture is one of massive continuity throughout the interwar period: both fragmentation and polarization remained low to moderate. A slight increase in fragmentation and polarization can be noted in the course of the 1930s, but this can hardly be assigned any importance. As for cabinet duration, the first period was the most unstable one. Apart from that, Danish politics is characterized by high cabinet duration. In sum, Danish politics in the years between the world wars provides no case for the thesis about relative changes in party system fragmentation.

Sweden

	1921	1924	1928	1932	1936
N	6	7	6	7	6
F	0.73	0.71	0.73	0.71	0.69
A	6.7	6.5	6.5	6.5	8.1
P	73.0	75.7	74.7	73.9	72.6
FB	0.61	0.62	0.64	0.64	0.66
FS	0.23	0.09	0.15	0.14	0.17

	1921-24[a]	1924-28[b]	1928-32[c]	1932-36[d]	1936-39[e]
CabA	536	704	459	728	1171
CaB	536	704	459	728	1171

a) incl. Trygger res. Oct. 18, 1924 (election Sept. 19-21)
b) incl. Ekman res. Sept 26, 1928 (election Sept. 15-21)
c) incl. Hamrin res. Sept. 19, 1932 (election Sept. 17-18)
d) incl. Pehrsson of Bramstorp res. Sept. 23, 1936 (election Sept. 20)
e) only Hansson res. Dec. 13, 1939

Again, the variation in party system fragmentation is small, and the general picture is dominated by a high level of continuity. Sweden was moderately fragmented and not extremely polarized throughout the interwar years. It would be misleading to speak of any clear changes, but it can be noted that the 1936 election brought about a slight decrease in fragmentation.

Cabinet stability was moderate to high. Interestingly enough, the 1936 election is also followed by an increase in cabinet stability. This may look like a confirmation of the basic hypothesis; the limited change concerning fragmentation should, however, be borne in mind.

Norway

	1921	1924	1927	1930	1933	1936
N	7	8	7	6	8	6
F	0.80	0.81	0.74	0.75	0.70	0.69
A	4.0	3.6	5.6	5.2	5.8	7.8
P	52.7	54.0	61.3	58.7	66.0	70.1
FB	0.72	0.71	0.67	0.68	0.69	0.67
FS	0.34	0.54	0.18	0	0	0

	1921-24[a]	1924-28[b]	1928-31[c]	1931-1933[d]
CabA	364	831	596	324
CabB	364	831	596	324

	1933-35[e]	1935-40[f]
CabA	744	1851
CabB	744	1851

a) incl. Berge res. June 25, 1924 (election Oct. 21)
b) incl. Lykke res. Jan 20, 1928 (election Oct. 17, 1927)
c) incl. Mowinckel res. May 8, 1931 (election Oct. 20, 1931)
d) incl. Hunseid res. Febr. 25, 1933 (election Oct. 16, 1933)
e) only Mowinckel res. March 16, 1935 (election Oct. 19, 1936)
f) only Nygaardsvold res. April 9, 1940

The Norwegian *Storting* cannot be dissolved, and the date for parliamentary elections is fixed. Since none of the Norwegian cabinets resigned clearly in connection with an election, it is somewhat difficult to 'match' parliamentary periods and cabinets.

The parliamentary party system went from a high to a moderate degree of fragmentation in the course of the interwar period. There was a decrease in the second half of the 1920s which continued becoming most marked after the 1936 election. Most of this change was due to the unification of the Left, leading in 1930 to the disappearance of the communists from the parliamentary scene. This process also entailed a higher level of polarization in the party system.

Cabinet duration varied considerably, ranging from low to very high. The lowest period in the early 1930s coincided with intermediate values of fragmentation, but cabinet duration was also comparatively short in the beginning of the period, when fragmentation was highest. More significantly, the least fragmented period in the second half of the 1930s more or less coincided with the Nygaardsvold cabinet, which sat for all of five years.

Although not a very strong case, Norway seems to lend some support to the hypothesis about the importance of relative changes in fragmentation.

Finland

	1919	1922	1924	1927	1929	1930	1933	1936	1939
N	6	6	6	6	6	6	8	8	7
F	0.75	0.80	0.79	0.79	0.78	0.75	0.76	0.74	0.71
A	6.7	4.4	5.0	5.0	5.0	4.7	4.9	5.2	6.1
P	54.0	57.5	58.0	57.0	55.0	54.0	55.0	58.5	59.0
FB	0.75	0.72	0.71	0.68	0.64	0.67	0.73	0.73	0.69
FS	0	0.45	0.36	0.38	0.40	0	0	0	0

	1919-22[a]	1922-24[b]	1924-29[c]	1929-32[d]
CabA	277	243	322	246
CabB	277	243	322	246

	1932-36[e]	1936-39[f]
CabA	1410	459

CabB 1410   459

a) incl. Vennola res. June 2, 1922 (election July 1-3)
b) incl. Cajander res. May 31, 1924 (election April 1-2)
c) incl. Mantere res. Aug. 16, 1929 (election July 1-2)
d) incl. Sunila res. Dec. 14, 1932 (election July 1-3)
e) only Kivimäki res. Oct. 7, 1936 (election July 1-2)
f) incl. Cajander res. Dec. 1, 1939

The fragmentation of the Finnish party system was moderate to high through the entire interwar period; a slight decrease took place at the very end of the period. Polarization and the fragmentation of the nonsocialist camp varied relatively little. By contrast, the disappearance of the communists from the Finnish parliament in 1930 created a wholly new situation on the Left, where the social democrats were the only contender up until 1945.

Until the first years of the 1930s, cabinet stability was low in Finland, with a similarly low degree of personal continuity. From 1932 onwards cabinet stability was moderate to high, Kivimäki's cabinet (1932-36) lasting nearly four years. Surely, there was no preceding change in party system fragmentation *at large* that could account for this change. If anything, the increased cabinet duration might be attributed to the consolidation of the left wing.

Intra-country processes: conclusions

This part of our study looked for any connections between *relative changes* in party system variables on the one hand, and cabinet stability and the ultimate fate of democracy on the other. The logic of this inquiry called for separate time-series analyses for each country.

The results can best be summarized separately for those countries where democracy broke down and for those in which it survived the crisis. Starting with the five countries which belonged to the former group, a common characteristic can be noted: cabinet instability, generally high in these countries, become even more pronounced immediately before the breakdown of democracy. This is clearly the case in all five countries, although the change is rather modest in Austria. This finding is, of course, hardly surprising. It may, nevertheless, be taken as an indication of some kind of a critical threshold. It is when cabinet stability goes *from bad to worse* that democracy itself is placed at risk.

At the same time, it is obvious that the five countries form anything but a homogeneous group as concerns relative changes in the party systemic variables. Table 6 is an attempt to summarize the significance of these changes. This is far from an exact analysis. Primarily, it takes the changes preceding the breakdown of democracy into account. However, an attempt is also made to assess the relationship between the independent variables and cabinet duration in general. A positive sign means that changes in an independent variable clearly relate to the dependent variables as predicted by the theory. Parentheses indicate that the changes were slight but went in the right direction. A zero means that neither positive nor negative connections could be discerned. A minus indicates that the empirical evidence runs counter to the theoretical expectations; parentheses are again used to indicate that this relationship is rather weak.

The 'theoretical expectations' are of course as follows: increases in the number of parties (N) and fractionalization (F, FB and FS) are expected to lead to increased instability. Increases in party aggregation (A) are expected to lead to increased stability. Increased polarization (P) is expected to lead to increased instability.

Table 6. Five cases of 'breakdown'. Summary of relationships between changes in party systemic variables and changes in political stability

	N	F	A	P	FB	FS
Italy	+	(+)	(+)	(+)	(+)	+
Germany	0	(-)	-	+	-	(+)
Austria	(+)	(+)	(+)	0	(+)	0

Estonia	-	-	-	0	-	(-)
Latvia	(-)	0	0	-	0	0

The emerging picture is disheartening from the point of view of our hypothesis. The two Baltic countries defy the theory completely; especially the Estonian case simply challenges it on almost all points. The increased instability and the eventual breakdown of Estonian democracy in the mid-1930s was preceded by *decreased* fragmentation of the party system. Even for the remaining three countries, the patterns vary considerably. The Italian case is most promising from the point of view of the theory, albeit the explanatory power of party system changes is generally weak. Except for the fractionalization of the left wing, the fragmentation measures run counter to the theory even in the German case; here, however, the impact of increasing polarization in the wake of the rise to prominence of the nazis seems to offer a potential explanation. Finally, in the Austrian case one may speak of 'low to no association', but at least the changes do not directly challenge the basic hypothesis.

Concerning the idea that increased fragmentation *above some critical threshold* might offer an explanation, the conclusion must be similarly negative. Those two cases that least contradict the basic hypothesis - Italy and Austria - are the *least* fragmented of the five cases of 'breakdown'.

As for the cases of 'survival', the interest i naturally directed toward possible connections between party system changes and peaks in cabinet instability. For the reasons mentioned above, Switzerland is omitted from Table 7, in which these connections are summarized.

Table 7. Ten cases of 'survival'. Summary of relationships between changes in party systemic variables and changes in political stability

	N	F	A	P	FB	FS
England	(+)	+	+	0	0	0
Ireland	(+)	(+)	(+)	(+)	0	0

France	+	+	+	0	+	-
Belgium	+	+	+	0	+	+
Netherlands	-	0	(-)	(+)	0	(-)
Czechosl.	(-)	(-)	0	0	0	0
Denmark	-	0	-	0	0	0
Sweden	(+)	(+)	(+)	(+)	0	0
Norway	0	+	+	(-)	0	(+)
Finland	-	(+)	0	0	0	+

As was to be expected, also the larger group of 'survivors' turns out to be quite heterogeneous with respect to the relationship between party system characteristics and variations in cabinet stability. In the cases of Belgium and France, changes in fragmentation largely seem to coincide with corresponding variations in cabinet stability. There is something of a similar pattern for England and Norway as well, although it is more ambiguous especially in the latter case. The relationship has the expected sign for Ireland and Sweden as well but remains rather weak in both cases. As for Finland, only the strengthening of the cohesion on the Left would seem to clearly match the expectations.

The remaining three cases - the Netherlands, Czechoslovakia and Denmark - are more or less disheartening. What there are of relationships mostly contradicts the theoretical expectations. Clearly, relative changes in party systemic variables do not offer and explanation of variations in political stability in these countries.

Again, the idea of 'critical thresholds' of fragmentation fails to gain empirical support. Of the three most 'positive' cases, England displays a low general level of fragmentation, Belgium is moderately fragmented, wheras fragmentation is generally high in France. Similarly, Ireland and Sweden differ clearly from each other as to the general level of party system fragmentation. Clearly, whatever the impact of changes in party system fragmentation on cabinet stability may have been in the individual cases, it was not dependent on some minimal level of fragmentation to start with.

All in all, relative changes in party system fragmentation seem to possess limited explanatory power pertaining to changes in political stability in individual countries. A minority of our cases appear to comply with the theory reasonably well, others are highly ambiguous, while the remainder more or less contradict the theoretically derived expectations. It is notable that the cases where this 'theory' fits best are to be found among the survivors rather than among the cases of 'breakdown'.

Our most important findings can be briefly summarized in the following way:

1 Cabinet stability went from low to very low immediately prior to the breakdown of democracy.

2 There is no 'critical threshold' of party system fragmentation above which increases in fragmentation lead to clear increases in cabinet or constitutional instability.

3 Relative changes in party systemic factors possess limited explanatory power vis-à-vis political stability. They more frequently coincide with changes in stability in those countries where democracy survived than in those where democracy went under.

Conclusions

Was the fragmentation of party systems a cause of government instability and ultimately of the breakdown of democracy in interwar Europe? Did polarization in conjunction with multipartism play a role? Was the fragmentation of the left wing particularly detrimental to the stability of the democratic system?

The most justifiable answer is perhaps the less desirable one: yes and no. If we combine the results of our two alternative tests of the 'fragmentation thesis', the following general picture emerges.

Table 8. Summary of two tests of the fragmentation thesis.

**Is cabinet stability/
the fate of democracy
explicable in terms of:**

		The general level of fragmentation?	
		Yes	No
Relative changes in fragmentation?	Yes	England Ireland Sweden Norway (Italy)	Austria France (Belgium)
	No	Estonia Latvia Germany Denmark	Czechoslovakia Netherlands (Finland)

Since cabinet stability is a necessary element of this table, Switzerland is again excluded. Italy, Belgium and Finland constitute borderline cases for the reasons dicussed in connection with Table 5.

Table 8 itself might give cause to either a pessimistic or an optimistic interpretation. The pessimist would point to the fact a clear minority of the cases comply with both aspects of fragmentation theory. The optimist would rather stress that only three (or maybe just two) of the cases seem totally insensitive to both aspects of the theory.

England, Ireland, Sweden and Norway remained below the median level of party system fragmentation. Moreover, their cabinet stability seems to have increased as a consequence of decreased fragmentation over time. Italy is a less clearcut case, but basically it constitutes a mirror image of these four countries. The Austrian case, not explicable in terms of the general *level* of fragmentation, displays an *increase* of fragmentation prior to the authoritarian takeover. The consolidation of the political blocs in France would seem to offer a potential solution to the enigma present in Table 5. Belgium is a borderline case as to the general level of fragmentation. Its cabinet stability, nevertheless, seems to vary according to relative changes in party system fragmentation. Estonia and Germany became rather *less* fragmented immediately before the collapse of democracy but they remained at the high general level of fragmentation typical of them throughout the period. In Latvia there was simply too little variation in fragmentation to justify any conclusions in this respect; the Latvian party system at all times remained the most fractionalized one in our sample of countries. The Danish level of fragmentation remained relatively low and the cabinet stability increased rather independently of the changes in fragmentation. Finally, Czechoslovakia, Netherlands and less clearly Finland defy both explanations. The two first countries were highly fragmented and relatively stable, and they displayed little connections between cabinet stability and relative changes in fragmentation. Finland was just on the border between high and low general level of fragmentation. Cabinet stability was generally low, but increased in the 1930s without any clear consolidation of the party system at large.

The above summary is based on the main dimensions of party system fragmentation (number of parties, fractionalization and party system aggregation). The fractionalization of the left wing and the nonsocialist bloc seems to add little to this general picture, and the same goes for polarization. True, all cases of 'breakdown' except Austria had fractionalized left as well as nonsocialist wings, but something like half of the cases of 'survival' had that as well. The increased polarization of the German party system is an oft-mentioned factor accounting for the collapse of democracy; on the other hand the rest of our material shows practically no association between party system polarization, instability and breakdown. Similarly, it would be tempting to attribute the increased stability and the eventual survival of Finnish democracy to the consolidation of the left wing. However, in the general European comparison this explanation falls rather short.

All five cases of 'breakdown' were generally unstable democracies, and their cabinet stability decreased immediately prior to the collapse of democratic rule. Four of the five cases had generally high levels of party system fragmentation. Indeed, they were 'paradigmatic cases' through the combination of party system fragmentation, low cabinet stability and the eventual breakdown of democracy.

All cases of generally high cabinet stability were among the 'survivors' among interwar European democracies. In other words, the interwar crisis did not destabilize previously stable regimes to a decisive degree. Indeed, as Linz has pointed out (1978, 5-8), 'stability bred stability' in Europe between the world wars. Save for one country (Austria), all cases of generally low party system fragmentation were among the 'survivors'. A majority of them combined low fragmentation with high levels of cabinet stability.

Yes, clearly party system fragmentation must be regarded as *one* major factor behind the outcome of interwar European politics. But no, it does not constitute an overshadowing explanation the way some of the early literature seems to suggest. Why did segmented states such as Czechoslovakia with a very high level of party system fragmentation remain comparatively stable while Latvia, similarly segmented and fractionalized, succumbed to autoritarian pressures? What was the crucial difference between Finland and Estonia, which not only share political instability and party system fragmentation but also a host of geographical, historical and cultural features? How come Austria, with its concentrated party system suffered from chronical instability finally leading to the collapse of democracy while France, seemingly hopelessly fragmented and unstable, managed to weather the interwar crisis? It is to these kinds of questions that we turn in our second set of empirical analyses.

Chapter 4

Consociationalism?
Pairwise comparisons

A typical feature of political science theory-building is that ideas labeled or marketed as 'theories' more frequently challenge the outlooks or perspectives of previous theories than the substative generalizations arrived at on the basis of the theories. Theories are like eyeglasses with lenses of varying colors: they help us see the world in a new light, but they do not necessarily correct previous conclusions. What is sometimes called theoretical advances in political science is not necessarily accompanied by falsification of previously presented empirical generalizations. Analyses of 'power' are followed by 'systems theory', which in turn gives way to 'postmodernism'. It is difficult to pinpoint corresponding breakthroughs in our empirical understanding of things political. The problem is simply that too few theorists have bothered to challenge the *factual* implications of previous theoretical work.

Arend Lijphart's work on consociationalism (or consensus democracy, as he prefers to call it today), has the advantage of clearly challenging the empirical implications of a large and central body of theoretical literature. In simplified terms, we may speak of an early post-WWII literature which sees the majoritarian model of democracy based on a two-party system as superior to multiparty systems with proportional representation. The former is supposed to more effectively secure the efficient functioning of the democractic system and thus constitute a better guarantee for the continued vitality of democracy. Lijphart is out to prove that such a generalization is incorrect in the light of systematic empirical examination. The stability of democratic regimes can be guaranteed in several different ways; those dimensions underlined in the earlier literature are not necessarily the critical ones conditioning the functioning and survivability of democracy.

Lijphart does not directly deny the importance of the factors - electoral systems, government structures, cabinet stability, and so on - which are stressed by those authors whom he wishes to challenge. Rather, he underlines the existence of a number of mechanisms which can check and counterbalance the effects of these factors. Again in rather simplified terms, one might say that the early literature stressed the *technical* aspects of political and constitutional arrangements; some arrangements - notably electoral systems based on plurality - were simply better in a purely objective technical sense than some others. Lijphart, by contrast, stresses the importance of the *social environment* in which such arrangements are to function. Majoritarian systems are functional in countries with few politically salient cleavages. By contrast, in plural societies

> - societies that are sharply divided along religious, ideological, linguistic, cultural, ethnic, or racial lines into virtually separate subsocieties with their own political parties, interest groups, and media of communication - the flexibility necessary for majoritarian democracy is absent. Under these conditions, majority rule is not only undemocratic but also dangerous, because minorities that are continually denied access to power will feel excluded and discriminated against and will lose their allegiance to the regime...
> In plural societies, therefore, majority rule spells majority dictatorship and civil strife rather than democracy (1984, 22-23).

The contrast to F.A. Hermens is as clear as one might possibly hope. Writing on the differences between two-party and multiparty systems, Hermens stresses that the parties in the former must be

> tolerant because they contain[] members of all major social and religious groups in their own ranks. We might call this process 'intra-party integration', and re-emphasize, in passing, that the maintenance of any large party is a never-ending task, as the various elements which compose it must again and again be reconciled with one another on the basis of a common denominator which is bound to shift in the process (1958, 176).

Multiparty systems, by contrast, are based on 'rigid principles'; when these are taken as seriously as some people want to take them, they become 'isms'. Parties develop into political sects and, instead of 'bickering' with each other in comparative safety, they lead a kind of holy war against each other (1958, 177).

Although more clearly a 'challenger' in terms of empirical conclusions than what is normally the case with 'contending approaches' in political science, Lijphart does not directly reject the main empirical evidence presented by Hermens and his contemporaries. Rather, he points to the narrowness and eclecticism present in the examples solicited in support of the 'two-party theory'. To be sure, it is difficult to deny that the British party system has provided for relative stability in British politics. By the same token, the American parties are arenas for a constant reconciliation of numerous diverging interests - or for 'intra-party integration', as Hermens puts it. Aall the same, these examples do not count as more than one each in the universe of democracies. By selecting other examples one may point to quite different effects of party systems.

On the one hand, majoritarian systems may, given certain social conditions, be dysfunctional and even threaten the basis of democratic rule itself. Lijphart cites the case of Northern Ireland, where the Protestant majority won every election and held executive power continuously between 1921 and 1972. This was a central factor in the process whereby the Catholic minority was alienated from the political system, and it finally drove Catholic militants to take up the armed struggle against the majority (1984, 23).

On the other hand, by shifting the focus from the large countries to the smaller democracies one may easily detect that majoritarian systems are not a necessary condition for a stable and continued democratic rule. True, most of the unstable democracies are to be found among the characteristic continental multiparty systems. All the same, most such systems are stable and democracy seems to have survived in them without any major difficulty.

In the previous chapter, a major dimension of this theoretical discussion was put to a systematic empirical test. The results, by no means unambiguous, indicated that the fragmentation of the party systems generally made it more difficult to secure the stable functioning of democracy. Therefore, it can be seen as one element necessary for understanding the fate of democracy in interwar Europe. Nevertheless, some very notable exceptions to this rule remain to be explained. It is to these puzzles we wish to turn with the help of the theory of consociational democracy.

Consociationalism: dimensions and operationalizations

Lijphart's two main works, *Democracy in Plural Societies* (1977) and *Democracies* (1984) have different points of departure, and in some respects the author's views have shifted somewhat over the years. Nevertheless, these two books and the numerous articles and special reports which complement them still form a coherent and basically continuous theoretical and empirical line.

The first book and the research connected to it aimed at outlining the phenomenon of consociational democracy and at pinpointing the social conditions which explained the emergence of consociational mechanisms in politics. 'What does consociationalism look like?' and 'how does it come about?' were the main questions. Certainly, the critique of the unquestioned superiority of majoritarianism was clearly present in this work. Nevertheless, there was a strong focus on the social structures behind political and party systems, and much of the criticism was directed against those authors who had sought to explain the social conditions for stable democratic rule, notably Gabriel Almond.

The second book, by contrast, is directly focused on political organization and party systems. Naturally, it cannot help but touch upon the social foundations of various political systems as well, as the very point in Lijphart's work is that there has to be a congruency between the political framework and the social structure of a society. Nevertheless, the shift of focus as compared to the 1977 book is rather clear. Moreover, Lijphart now directly starts out from the basic tenets of majoritarian democracy - or the 'Westminster Model', as he calls it. By critically examining its premises and by contrasting it to his alternative 'Consensus Model', he creates a direct confrontation between two competing theories of political and institutional organization. Thus, in the second book the character of consociationalism as a 'challenger' is quite marked.

The present study is, as was pointed out at the beginning of Chapter I, based on the conviction that it is of primary importance to examine political factors when looking for explanations to political pehomena. Consequently, our focus comes clearly closer to Lijphart's second than his first book. In other words, when discussing the explanatory power of the theory of consociationalism we focus on political mechanisms associated with consociationalism rather than on the social preconditions of those mechanisms. Again, the discussion naturally cannot be carried out in a vacuum, and social structures will frequently be referred to in the course of the analysis. Nevertheless, from a principal point of view they are not a necessary element in the theoretical investigation. The question is: *do consociational mechanisms explain crucial differences in political and constitutional stability in cases that do not appear explicable in terms of party system fragmentation?* In other words: are there systematic differences between such cases concerning consociational mechanisms, and can it be demonstrated that these mechanisms were related to the way in which the interwar crisis evolved? By contrast, we will *not* pay systematic attention to the question of whether these mechanisms in fact emerged due to the social factors underlined by Lijphart as central preconditions.

Consociational mechanisms: dimensions

The central element in a consociational democracy separating it from a majoritarian democracy is the propensity for *elite cooperation*. A majoritarian democracy means competing political elites alternating in power. A consociational democracy means cooperating political elites constantly seeking formulas for the sharing of power. In a majoritarian democracy, the majority rules over the minority, the 'winners' of an election take power over the 'losers'. In consociational democracy, there are no majorities, only smaller or larger minorities; one does not win or lose *an* election, one simply makes gains or losses *in* an election.

In his first book, Lijphart identified four basic characteristics of consociational democracy: *grand coalition, segmental autonomy, proportionality, and minority veto*. Writing on 'consensus democracy' seven years later, he had increased the number of dimensions to eight. According to him, the original four characteristics of consociational democracy are 'clearly recognizable in, but not coincident with, the eight characteristics of consensus democracy' (1984, xiv). In the present study, this latter list of characteristics forms the framework according to which our comparative case studies will be structured.

1 Executive power-sharing: grand coalitions. This first characteristic represents perhaps the most fundamental contrast between consociational and majoritarian systems. Instead of competing for exclusive government power, all major parties share power according to a certain formula, be it an officially codified rule or an informal practice. This formula may be sensitive to election results so as to permit shifts in the relative representation of the various parties. At all times, however, it guarantees a minimum share of executive power to the parties representing the main segments of the society, be they linguistic, religious or regional groups. Lijphart illustrates this mechanism with examples from post-WWII Switzerland and Belgium, the two countries which constitute his master cases of consensus democracy.

2 Separation of powers, formal and informal. The Montesqueian principle of the institutional separation of political authority is not only practiced in the United States. Lijphart argues that the Swiss system of fixed-term Federal Councils has a similar effect. Although the Federal Council is elected by the legislature, it is subsequently basically immune to pressures on the part of the parliament, because the latter cannot vote it out of office. Compared to the majoritarian systems of Britain and New Zealand, this makes for a much more balanced relationship between the two main branches of government.

In addition to this formal separation of powers, Lijphart stresses the importance of informal arrangements that may serve the same purpose. Thus, 'Belgian cabinets, largely because they are often broad and uncohesive coalitions, are not at all as dominant as their British counterparts, and they tend to have a genuine give-and take relationship with parliament' (1984, 25). In other words, Lijphart directs attention to cases that, without a formal separation of powers, have an 'executive-legislative relationship that may be regarded as an informal or semiseparation of powers' (Ibid.)

3 Balanced bicameralism and minority representation. Bicameralism is, of course, a common feature among the world's democracies; even the British system of parliament, although perceived as the very antonym of a consociational system, is a bicameral one. However, Lijphart stresses that the existence of two chambers is as such insufficient as a guarantee of consociational elements in the political system. The two chambers must be chosen on different bases so as to ensure the representation of different aspects of social life. Usually this means that one of the chambers provides for straightforward 'numeric' representation, while the other secures regional representation; other criteria, such as linguistic or religious cleavages, can constitute the basis as well. Moreover, both chambers must have real power in the sense that none of them is overwhelmingly superior to the other. Again, Lijphart's two master cases stand in a clear contrast to, i.a., the British system entirely dominated by the Lower House of the Parliament.

4 Multiparty system. This dimension needs little elaboration. It simply denotes the existence of more than two parties of central importance to the legislative and executive politics of a country.

5 Multidimensional party system. This dimension is of course closely connected with the previous one. It need not, however, be identical with it: even   multiparty systems can be structured largely according to the socioeconomic left-right scale. The multidimensionality of the party systems means that there are other important cleavages conditioning the party system besides the economy: religion, language, culture and region are the main types of cleavages that can permanently affect the structuring of political alternatives in the form of parties.

6 Proportional representation. Largely in line with Hermens and others, Lijphart sees a connection between multipartism and proportional representation. His description of the effects of PR is, however, entirely different from Hermens' unequivocally negative view: '...that their proportional electoral systems have not inhibited the translation of societal cleavages into party system cleavages' (1984, 28).

7 Territorial and nonterritorial federalism and decentralization. Normally, federalism means territorial autonomy of the kind that is well known from, i.a., Switzerland and the United States. There is a division of power between the central government and regional governments; the latter must have full powers in a wide variety of important political and social fields. Lijphart emphasizes, however, that nonterritorial arrangements providing for, e.g., cultural autonomy, are potentially just as important as expressions of federalism and political decentralization. He mentions the cultural councils of the Walloon and Flemish communities in Belgium as examples of such cultural and linguistic autonomy. Although not directly territorial, such arrangements challenge the hierarchical geographic pattern of a strictly unitary model, and they may have far-reaching effects on the political process as well.

8 Written constitution and minority veto. In contradistinction to the majoritarian systems of Great Britain and New Zealand, Belgium and Switzerland have written constitutions, 'single document[s] containing the basic rules of governance' (1984, 29). In both cases, the constitution can be changed only if special majorities support the amendment. In the Swiss case, the smaller cantons are especially protected in connection with constitutional change; in many ways, the Swiss constitution is designed so as to safeguard the territorial dimension of Swiss politics. By the same token, the qualified majorities necessary for constitutional amendments in Belgium largely aim at protecting the cultural autonomy of the two linguistic groups. In fact, any group mustering a third of the parliamentary seats controls an effective minority veto in Belgian politics. This not only applies to formally constitutional matters but also those questions where the cultural autonomy of one of the groups is at stake.

In addition to these eight characteristics, Lijphart also discusses direct democracy in relation to majoritarianism and consensus democracy. An oft-mentioned characteristic of majoritarian democracy is that it is exclusively representative. On the other hand Switzerland, the consociational democracy *par excellence*, has an entirely unique record of referendum democracy. This might lead one to believe that institutional expressions of direct democracy are a feature of consociational systems more generally.

This is, however, not the case. There is no systematic difference between majoritarian and plural systems pertaining to the use of referenda. Lijphart concludes that direct democracy can not be seen as either 'typically majoritarian or typically consensual. In fact, it is a foreign element in both majoritarian and consensus democracy because it is the antithesis of representative democracy' (1984, 32).

Comments

Lijphart's list of characteristics provides an outline for an *ideal type* of consensus democracy. This is to say that he does not expect to find a definite dividing line between those countries that are consociational and others that are majoritarian. In fact, even his 'master cases' - Belgium and Switzerland - differ from each other on several important points on his list. If the dimensions of consociationalism are applied with great rigidity, not even these countries represent 'pure' consensus democracy. Similarly, majoritarian democracy is an ideal model rather than a definite category of political systems.

All this goes to say that the question of consociationalism versus majoritarianism is one of degree rather than kind; Lijphart himself speaks of a *continuum* on which regimes can occupy varying positions (1984, 32). The operational consequence for research is, on the one hand, that two types of problems can occur. First, it may be difficult to determine critical cutting points on the various dimensions: 'so much x is means consociationalism, anything less than that is majoritarianism'. This is no small problem, but critical values of this kind can normally be stipulated in social and political research. A potentially more vexing problem is the fact that countries may display 'inconsistent' combinations of variable values: they may take on typically 'consociational' values on some dimensions and 'majoritarian' positions on others. Such a 'dissonance' can be very difficult to judge if the ambition is to clearly rank cases on the two main dimensions.

These problems are quite apparent in Lijphart's own analysis. His solution is a relativistic one, as he employs continuous or at least trinary variables to measure most of his dimensions. Consequently, most countries occupy more or less intermediary positions on the continuum, although the empirical data clearly point to the existence of relatively consistent majoritarian and consensual groups as well.

The lesson for further empirical study is, therefore, that some 'degreeism' will be necessary if one wishes to use the theory of consociationalism. In the present study, Lijphart's dimensions and several of his empirical solutions will be used as a framework for comparisons. At the same time, it is equally important to try and determine to what extent these dimensions were actually conducive to the crucial actions taken by political leaders in interwar Europe.

Empirical analysis: pairwise comparisons

The analysis of party system fragmentation and cabinet stability above left us with a number of cases which appear puzzling in the light of the theoretical framework applied in that part of the book. The following section discusses the selection of cases to be analyzed in the light of Lijphart's model. Methodological aspects will also be included in this discussion.

Cases, methods and data

The analysis of party systemic factors with the aid of aggregate data at the cross-national level indicated that such factors are clearly relevant but far from sufficient as explanations of government and constitutional stability in interwar Europe. Bivariate analyses pointed at best to weak-to-moderate association between party system variables and the level of stability. When party system fragmentation, cabinet stability and the final regime outcome were combined, almost half of the countries turned out to be intermediate cases between the paradigmatic types: 'the weakly fragmented stable democracy that survived' and 'the highly fragmented unstable system that collapsed'. Austria, Belgium, Czechoslovakia, Finland, France, the Netherlands and Switzerland belonged, to various degrees, to the group in between these extremes.

The attempt to complement this analysis by appraising the effects of relative changes of party system fragmentation within individual countries gave largely unsatisfactory results. In a clear majority of cases, such dramatic changes as would have merited definite conclusions simply did not occur; what was worse, in some cases *contrary* developments took place. Czechoslovakia, to a lesser extent Finland and the Netherlands still stood out as definite 'puzzles'.

This part of our study attempts to explore the dynamics of the interwar period more in depth. The extensive research strategy present in the first empirical analysis will give way to a more intensive mode of research. Not just static characteristics of political systems but also their interplay with the actions and decisions of political elites will be at the center of attention. This goes to say that a more qualitative analysis is called for. This, in turn, restricts the number of cases that can be accommodated within the framework of the study.

The study comprises six different countries, studied within the framework of *three pairwise comparisons*. Two of the pairs readily suggest themselves, and they in many ways seem to come close to a 'most similar case-analysis'. Czechoslovakia and Latvia form the first pair, Finland and Estonia the second one. In both of these pairs, the countries share similarities on the dimensions of the fragmentation theory plus a wide range of other common factors of social, cultural and historical character. The third pair is more difficult to give a methodological label. It would certainly be an exaggeration to describe France and Austria as a case of 'most different systems-design'. Rather, what is fascinating about them is that they both so clearly contradict the basic idea about party system fragmentation. Given the level of fragmentation, French democracy 'should have' collapsed; similarly, Austrian democracy 'should have' survived. The question is whether consociational mechanisms are the key to this riddle.

As for the empirical material, this part of our study is largely based on secondary sources. Most of the facts needed here are in themselves neither highly controversial or particularly difficult to come by. What is new about this inquiry is rather the theoretical context in which these data are examined.

For all the countries, more detailed descriptions of basic similarities and differences in their backgrounds will be presented at the outset of each case study.

Czechoslovakia and Latvia

Czechoslovakia and Latvia form perhaps the most puzzling couple among our cases. Their party systems were extreme in their fractionalization. Latvia had between 22 and 28 parties in the *saeima* between 1922 and 1934; the level of fractionalization (F) ranged between 0.87 and 0.92. Somewhat fewer (14-17) parties were represented in the Czechoslovakian parliament; still fractionalization was at the same level as in Latvia, ranging from 0.85 to 0.93 between 1920 and 1938. The two countries were, moreover, largely similar also as concerns the other party systemic variables included in the first part of our study.

Furthermore, the countries shared other characteristic features as well. They were both 'successor states' having emerged from the postwar settlement after the fall of the Habsburg and Russian empires, respectively. More notably, they were both multiethnic societies. In Czechoslovakia no ethnic or linguistic group had the absolute majority of the population. The Czechs came close to that, but the combined shares of Germans, Slovaks, Hungarians, Ruthenians, Poles and other minor nationalities amounted to more than fifty per cent of the population. The Latvians, by contrast, formed a reasonably clear (over seventy per cent) majority in their country. Still, Russians, Germans, Poles, Lithuanians represented important minorities not just in a local but to a large extent in a national context. Moreover, in both countries there was a large Jewish population.

The political process and the final outcome of interwar politics stands in a sharp contrast to these similarities. To be sure, the complicated party settings and social and ethnic structures created largely similar political issues in the two countries. Still, at all times Czechoslovakia managed its internal political situation more successfully than Latvia. Although by no means extremely stable, Czechoslovakian cabinets lasted a little longer than the overall average for all cabinets in interwar Europe. Latvia, by contrast, was clearly below this average. More importantly, of course, Czechoslovakia managed to remain democratic until the pressure from Hitler's Germany led to the dissolution of the Czechoslovakian state. To be sure, at times the internal situation was extremely complicated, and Hitler's intervention was aided by these internal pressures. Nevertheless, it was external intervention that put an end to

Czechoslovak democracy. In Latvia, by contrast, the authoritarian takeover in 1934 bore a clear domestic stamp.

Executive power-sharing: grand coalitions

At the outset, the *Czechoslovak* Republic seemed to be headed for anything but 'executive power-sharing' between the main segments of the society. The new state proposed by Masaryk and his adherents looked like a national state of the Czechs and Slovaks; the prevailing wish among the Germans seemed to be to become part of German-speaking Austria.

The National Committee (*Národni Vybor*) created on October 28, 1918 as well as the Revolutionary Assembly to which the Committee transferred all legislative powers were made up of representatives of Czechs and Slovaks only. This may have looked as a direct attempt to permanently exclude the Germans (and the Hungarians) from executive power. However, at several instances in connection with the drafting of the Czechoslovak constitution, German participation in government was considered. It was certainly not Masaryk's intention to design a political system which drew the minorities toward separatism (Bruegel 1973, 54-55).

Nevertheless, the first six years after the adoption of the constitution in 1920 were for all practical purposes a period of *Czech* executive power. Government coalitions with Social Democrats, National Socialists (a moderate left wing party in no way related to German national socialism), Agrarians and the clerical People's Party as central elements were the rule; Slovak participation was sporadic. The cabinets could initially rely on fairly reassuring majorities in the Chamber of Deputies (up to two-thirds of the parliamentary seats). However, the split of the Czech Social Democratic Party, leading to the foundation of the Czechoslovak Communist Party in October, 1921, weakened the cabinet coalition considerably. This party split led to the resignation of Wlastimil Tusar's cabinet and its replacement by a cabinet of civil servants under the leadership of Johann Cerny.

Executive politics based on 'coalition cabinets composed of parties which were ideologically and programmatically at cross-puposes with each other' (Hapala 1968, 134) was never a simple matter. With the split of the social democratic camp it became even more difficult. Although pressed by the rise of the communists, the social democrats as well as the other coalition partners continued to recognize the importance of maintaining a majority consensus in the political life. In order to safeguard the process of arriving at compromises the leaders of the five main parties formed the *Petka*, the Council of Five. The Petka was originally created to give political guidance to Cerny's non-political cabinet. It continued its activities even after the return of the composite parties to government position. In fact it is deemed to have been the real power center of the republic (Tingsten 1933, 652). Milan Hapala (1968, 134) puts it thus:

> The policy-making process which would ordinarily take place in the legislature, under cabinet leadership, was initiatied, and perhaps concluded, in the extra-constitutional committee of party leaders who came together to explore possibilities of action which transcended the ideological differences that separated them. The organization of the Petka was perhaps the most significant modification of governmental machinery by the parties.

The Petka was clearly a grand coalition in the sense of bridging both the left-right and the clerical anti-clerical gap. It was, however, a *Czech* grand coalition. Luebbert seems to be under the impression that both the Czech and German Social Democratic parties participated in the Petka 'for all but the years between 1925 and 1929' (Luebbert 1991, 291). This is, however, contradicted by other authors (Tingsten 1933, 652; Lijphart 1977, 33, footnote). Bruegel's detailed account (1973) of German participation in interwar Czechoslovakian politics says nothing about the German Social Democratic role in the Petka.

However, if the Petka and the cabinets did not bridge the gap between the nationalities in the first half of the 1920s, the cabinets that were to follow certainly did. From October, 1926 until the end of 1929, cabinets including all major Czech parties except the social democrats governed the country together with the German Christian Social and Agrarian Parties as well as the Slovak People's Party. In the following seven cabinets, the increasingly fascist Slovak People's Party was replaced by the Slovak Socialists (except in Johann Malypetr's short-lived third cabinet in 1935, which had no Slovak representation). The sizable German Social Democratic Party also took part in these cabinets accompanied by the German Agrarian Party. In the last cabinet before Munich (Milan Hodza's third cabinet) even the German Christian Socials took part. Meanwhile, all main Czech parties participated in the cabinets between 1929 and 1938. Consequently, these were strong majority cabinets, frequently controlling more than two-thirds of the parliamentary seats. Fascism and separatism grew stronger in both Slovakia and in German-speaking Sudetenland in the course of the 1930s, however. To be sure, Father Andrei Hlinka's Slovak People's Party never won the absolute majority of the Slovak vote. The Sudeten-German Nazis under Konrad Henlein could, however, claim to represent the majority of their people. Nevertheless, in terms of political cleavages the cabinet politics of the 1930s, particularly the period immediately before Munich indeed was a time of grand coalitions in Czechoslovakia: economic, religious as well as national divides were bridged in the executive branch of the government.

In the interim between the end of the Civil War in January 1920 and the adoption of the Constitution in February, 1922, *Latvia* was first governed by Karlis Ulmanis' cabinet which lacked the support of the Left altogether. However, in order to be able to draft a constitution which could win the majority of the Constituent Assembly a broader coalition including some of the members of the socialist left, together with Ulmanis' Agrarians as well as some other centrist parties was formed (Barr Carson 1956, 301).

The two basic cleavages to be bridged by Latvian coalitions were the left-right one and the ethnic-cultural one. Both turned out to be very problematic, and a coalition bridging both divides never came about.

Typical of Latvian government politics more or less throughout the interwar period was the predominance of the Peasant League under Ulmanis. Although the party never won more than sixteen of the 100 seats in the saeima, it was the center around which most Latvian cabinets came to revolve. Together with some minor rightist and centrist groups it commanded between thirty and forty per cent of the seats. Given the fifteen to twenty per cent belonging to the various national minority parties, it was possible to form majority cabinets without the Left Wing. However, these cabinets, which never commanded more than 51-56 per cent of the seats, were feeble indeed. The host of parties which made up the majority at all times entered cabinets on special conditions and tended to withdraw as soon as these conditions could not be met (von Rauch 1967, 92-93; Svabe 1961, 105-106; Tingsten 1933, 655).

The most volatile part of these coalitions were the parties representing the various national minorities. All of six different parties competed for the Russian vote, while there were five different Jewish fractions in the saeima. The only minority which managed to create a more or less unified party organization were the Germans. Michael Garleff offers a vivid description of the role of these groups in Latvian parliamentary politics around the mid 1920s:

> ...the spring of 1924 Russian and Jewish representatives supported the Zamuels cabinet in accord with other minority groups. A year later the German action supported the Celmins cabinet (December 19, 1924 - December 3, 1925). Russians, Jews and Poles remained neutral by not voting in matters which directly concerned the government. After the second German attempt to create a minority bloc failed, a portion of the minority parliamentarians began to cooperate more closely. Two Jewish, two Polish, and three Russian delegates formed a faction with the somewhat misleading name 'Democratic Bloc of Minorities', which leaned toward Left-of-Center Latvian parties. The three other Jewish delegates, though also 'democratically' inclined, tended to support the bourgeois coalition...(Garleff 1978, 92).

The crucial factor was, however, the position of the social democrats. The Latvian Social Democratic Party was clearly the largest party in the saeima, mustering at most 31 of the 100 seats. Its support fell in the course of the late 1920s and early 1930s; in the last 'free' saeima elected in 1931 it held merely twenty seats. The speaker of the parliament was at all times a social democrat (Svabe 1961, 105). However, the cabinet participation of this party was very limited, altogether comprising only approximately twenty months. In 1923, social democratic ministers took part in a coalition headed by J. Pauluks, a non-partisan Prime Minister. Three years later they participated in a coalition led by M. Skujenieks, the leader of the free-wheeling Right Wing Social Democratic fraction (Balodis 1990, 201; cf. Bilmanis 1934, 81). For all practical purposes, however, the social democrats were in permanent opposition. Most importantly, a coalition of social democrats and agrarians, which would have been *the* Latvian grand coalition, never came about.

In sum, although none of the two countries ever saw a coalition uniting all major parties, it is obvious that Czechoslovakia scored much higher on this dimension than Latvia.

Separation of powers, formal and informal

Czechoslovakia had a parliamentary system. This goes to say that the center of political power lay in the parliament and in the cabinet which was dependent on the will of the parliamentary majority. The Head of State was the President, but the constitution placed

> ..severe restrictions... on the Presidency which had been fashioned after the parliamentary system of the Third French Republic, with its weak figure-head type of Presidency (Táborsky 1968, 118).

This is a characterization which can be found in most descriptions of interwar Czechoslovakian government. As a statement concerning the formal constitutional framework it is entirely correct. The President was elected for a period of seven years by both chambers of the parliament. The suspensive power of veto he had in relation to the parliament was legally weak. A normal majority of the chambers was sufficient to break it. The President could, moreover, dissolve the parliament and call for new elections. All the same, the constitution clearly subordinated the Presidency to the parliament.

At the same time - and equally few authors forget this point - the Czechoslovak President, Thomas Masaryk in particular, had a political influence far beyond the constitutional confines of the Presidency. His role as a broker or *pouvoir neutre* between the various groups and parties was of paramount importance, and no serious politician really called his authority into question (see especially Coakley 1986, 196). Especially concerning the relations between the various ethnic parties and the question of German participation in cabinet coalitions, the role of Masaryk as well as of his successor Eduard Benes was decisive. Mohlin (1991, 69) notes the importance of the constitutional provision that allowed the re-election of the president; this gave Czechoslovak politics a degree of continuity beyond parliamentary politics and elections.

Moreover, the informal separation of powers between cabinet, parliament and the *Petka* should be noted in this context.

Similarly, *Latvia* is usually described in a rather uniform manner in the literature. Most authors not only characterize the Latvian form of government as parliamentary but 'hyper-parliamentary' or as an expression of radical parliamentarism. The Weimar Constitution was the model, and the saeima was wholly sovereign in relation to the other government institutions: 'The executive branch was completely dependent on unqualified legislative decisions, better described as whims' (Vardys 1978, 66).

The president, who was the formal Head of State, was elected by the parliament, not by popular vote. He could ask for a revision of parliamentary bills or suspend them for up to two months, but had, over and above this, no effective veto. He had the formal right to dissolve the parliament, but in order for this dissolution to be valid it had to be confirmed in a referendum; if the people then rejected the dissolution, the president had to resign. This elaborate procedure meant, of course, that the power of dissolution was all but a dead letter. Moreover, the president's influence was limited by the fact that he could be elected for a maximum of two three-year terms (Barr Carson 1956, 302).

Of much greater importance still was the fact that there was no person so generally respected by the various political camps that hew could have exerted a moderating power over the turbulent parliamentary scene. Attempts at revising the constitution in order to render the excutive branch of government more powerful were repeatedly voted down by the social democrats, who feared that such revisions would lead to the undue growth of the Peasant League's and Ulmanis' influence.

The final attempt was made in 1933. The Peasant League had proposed that the powers of the president be radically increased at the expense of the parliament; the original proposal would have brought Latvia close to an authoritarian model of government. The Committee on Social Rights to which it was submitted revised the proposal thoroughly reinstating much of the parliamentary influence, but still proposing that the president be elected by a direct popular vote and given an effective right to dissolve the saeima.

However, even in this form the reform was voted down at the plenary session, primarily by the Left. This was the definite impetus behind Ulmanis' decision to carry out a coup d'etat on May 15-16, 1934 (Svabe 1961, 106-107; Spekke 1951, 375; Vardys 1978, 75).

Again, Czechoslovakia clearly matches Lijphart's decsription of a consensus democracy better than Latvia. It should be stressed, however, that it was the informal role of the president (and the Petka) rather than the blueprint of the constitution that made for an effective separation of powers in Czechoslovakia as compared to Latvia.

Balanced bicameralism and minority representation

The *Czechoslovak* constitution was unequivocally 'Western' in the sense that the founding fathers of the Republic looked to the Anglo-Saxon world and to France and Belgium for models. Among the elements thus 'borrowed' was legislative bicameralism. In making a case for bicameralism, the Revolutionary Assembly pointed to the fact that these states that were the 'most civilized' nations of the world and therefore represented a model for the Czechoslovaks all had bicameral legislatures (Burian 1967, 93).

If, however, the intention of the founding fathers was to create a system of 'balanced bicameralism'- which is somewhat uncertain - the result was a far cry from this. The upper house (if this is the correct expression) of the parliament, the Senate, came to be clearly subordinate to the Chamber of Deputies. Its 150 members were, to be sure, to be elected for eight years, whereas the 300 Deputies sat a six-year period. Moreover, franchise was limited to citizens of 26 years of age and over; for the elections to the Chamber of Deputies, 21 years was the voting age. All the same, both chambers were elected by the same kind of popular vote based on proportionality. Consequently, the composition of the Senate in no marked way differed from that of the Chamber of Deputies; it did not form a basis for minority or regional representation over and above what was the case in the lower chamber. 'The center of gravity of the parliamentary work lie in the Chamber of Deputies' (Burian 1967, 94; cf. also Tingsten 1933, 650).

As for *Latvia: ex nihilo nihil.* Latvia had a unicameral representation; the saeima, elected for a three-year period through universal suffrage was the very core of political power in the Republic (e.g., Spekke 1951, 371-372).

Again, a difference between Czecholsovakia and Latvia can be noted so that the former comes closer to Lijphart's model than the latter. However, it must be stressed that none of the states comes anywhere near Lijphart's explicit requirement of *balanced* bicameralism.

The party system: parties and dimensions

The fact that both countries had extreme multiparty systems should be quite apparent by now. It is, therefore, not necessary to dwell on that dimension of Lijphart's model further. Instead, this section gives an account on the dimensions of the party systems and links the main parties to these dimensions.

In *Czechoslovakia*, economy, language and religion were the main cleavages underlying the party system. In some respects, they were reinforced by the regional-territorial dimension; to a large extent, however, they cut across it (cf. Burian 1967, 101; Hapala 1968, 124-140).

The Czech and German-speaking lands represented the most industrialized parts of the country (and indeed of Europe). Consequently, there were strong Czech and German social democratic parties which primarily represented the industrial working class. Before the party split in 1921 the Czech social democrats mustered a quarter of the total vote, thus being not only the strongest Czech party but the strongest party in the entire republic. As of the 1925 election their vote was, however, cut by half. The German social democrats were similarly dominant among the German-speaking voters at the beginning of the 1920s. They lost ground throughout the interwar period, however, and the 1935 election was a disaster from their point of view. They were down to less than four per cent of the vote, while the increasingly nazi *Sudetendeutsche Partei* won over fifteen per cent of the vote, being the electorally strongest party in the entire country.

In Slovakia, by contrast, the considerably lower degree of industrialization led to a weaker socialist support. Here, the clerical dimension was of paramount importance. Father Hlinka's Slovak People's Party largely throve on Slovak suspicion against the 'free-thinkers' and 'Hussites' of Bohemia. Its autonomist posture took on an increasingly separatist character, while at the same time the influence from Mussolini's Italy became clear in the 1930s. The Hlinka Party won up to forty per cent of the Slovak vote (Merkl 1980, 756) and it became instrumental to the dismantling of the Czechoslovak state after Munich (Nolte 1968, 243-244).

There were agrarian and Christian parties in both the Czech and German areas; these were all 'state-bearing' parties in the sense that they all participated in government coalitions at various times. The Czech Small Farmers' Party was particularly important, being one of the largest parties (up to fifteen per cent of the vote) in the country. Moreover, there was a Czech party representing small entrepreneurs; although small (2-5 per cent) it was an important part of the democratic consensus. Even more important was the Czech peculiarity, the National Socialist Party. This social radical party was in many ways at the core of the original Czech consensus; many leading Czech intellectuals, notably Eduard Benes, belonged to this party.

There were, in addition, Hungarian and Polish party formations, part of the former being of some national significance. Even here, the tendency was to organize several parties primarily according to socio-economic cleavages (Hapala 1968, 124-140).

The *Latvian* picture is not identical, but the similarities are still considerable (Bilmanis 1934, 79-80; Balodis 1990, 200-206). There is a strong social democratic party, much larger than any other party at the outset but declining over time. There is the multitude of ethnic parties, not just one but several parties for each minority. There is the large number of more or less nondescript centrist parties. Finally, there is an agrarian party with about fifteen per cent of the vote but with a central role in cabinet politics.

On the other hand, there really was no corresponding split of the socialist wing as the one that led to the establishment of the Czechoslovak Communist Party in 1921. To be sure, there was some turbulence on the Left in connection with the decline of the social democrats; still no party emerged as a permanent challenger on the Left. Moreover, the great number of small peasant parties - there were a total of six different agrarian groups besides Ulmanis' party represented in the saeima at various points in time - sets Latvia somewhat apart from Czechoslovakia.

The fragmentation of the Latvian minority parties was even more pronounced than the case was with Czechoslovakia. Only the Germans managed to overcome their internal differences and present a unified list in the elections. This was certainly of some significance. Of much more potential importance was the fact that the largest minority, the Russians, at all times remained hopelessly split. No less than six different parties competed for the Russian vote, and none of them ever won more than two seats in the parliament. Similarly, three to five Jewish parties competed with each other (Garleff 1978).

In a word, both countries were extreme multiparty systems based on a great number of partially cross-cutting societal cleavages.

Proportional representation

Both Czechoslovakia and Latvia had electoral systems based on the principle of proportionality. The *Czech* system was rather complicated. It was based on fixed-order lists determined by the political parties. In the first counting of votes seats were assigned on the basis of the total votes received by the various party lists. The second round was undertaken after the total votes had been divided by a quotient. In the second round only parties that had received at least 20,000 (elections to the Chamber of Deputies) or 35,000 votes (election to the Senate) in a constituency were included. (This was the system introduced in 1935; before that, another variant of the system was applied). Moreover, to be included in the second round a party had to win at least 120,000 votes at the national level. A third counting was undertaken if there still remained unassigned seats. The country was divided into 23 electoral districts for election to the Chamber of Deputies, while 12 districts were used for Senate elections (Hapala 1968, 135).

The system was party-centered in the sense that the fixed list system gave the party organizations considerable influence as to the persons who were actually elected as representatives. Moreover, it favored the Czech parties to some extent, while the German parties were slightly disfavored by the arithmetic of the electoral system (Burian 1967, 99).

Latvia can certainly be called an extreme case. Any group of seven citizens could form a party, and any group of 100 citizens could nominate a full slate of candidates in any electoral district (Barr Carson 1956, 303). The system was strictly proportional, and as there were only five electoral districts (Silde 1976, 344-345) the formation of small fractions was encouraged. The extreme proportionality of the electoral system was in fact one of the main themes of the discussion aiming at a constitutional revision, which, as we have seen above, never came about. The proliferation of small parties and the ensuing volatility of Latvian parliamentary politics certainly reflected actual societal cleavages; it is, however, clear that the electoral system played a central role by *allowing* these cleavages come to play in an almost totally unrestricted way.

Both countries thus match this dimension of the Lijphart model. Latvia surely is the extreme case.

Territorial and nonterritorial federalism and decentralization

The fact that interwar *Czechoslovakia* is frequently described as 'the Switzerland of the East' is in a way paradoxical. Certainly, Czechoslovakia managed to strike a certain balance between the nationalities in the course of the two decades between the world wars. Still, the most 'Swiss' of the ideas in the Pittsburg agreement of 1918 between the Czechs and the Slovaks, that of regional autonomy, never became reality.

The idea of regional autonomy came to clash with the principle of democracy and socio-economic equality as well as with the more concrete question of Sudeten-German separatism. A federal system would most probably have led to a cementation of the considerable social and economic differences between the industrialized and highly developed Czech lands on the one hand and Slovakia and Carpato-Ruthenia on the other. In fact it is conceivable that democracy as such would have become precarious in these less developed areas within a framework of regional autonomy (Lemberg 1967, 118).

As for the Germans, they had declared their wish to join Austria after the fall of the Empire. They came to be regarded as a foreign element during the formative years of Czechoslovak independence. (From a geo-political point of view, the idea of joining the Sudentenland with Austria was in fact rather unrealistic, since large parts of it did not border on Austria at all.)

So regional autonomy there was not, but the multi-cultural situation must me handled with in some fashion. The 1920 Constitution explicitly

> guaranteed the free use of their national language to everyone, schools for national minorities with instruction given in their own language and appropriate subsidies from public funds for cultural and other purposes (Bruegel 1973, 58).

A body of more specific legislation regulated the concrete administration of minority educational and cultural affairs; in this sense, there certainly was a degree of cultural decentralization in Czechoslovakia. Nevertheless, this at no time amounted to a comprehensive system of cultural autonomy. In fact, the language law enacted together with the Constitution had a principally discriminatory character, since it gave Czech and Slovak the status of national languages. Although of lesser practical importance, this affected the opinions of German nationalists. Characteristically enough, Masaryk expressed his displeasure with this Czechoslovak nationalist tendency in the language law (Bruegel 1973, 59-60).

Latvia was, in a pronounced manner, a unitary state. A federal structure was never seriously considered, and the debates on decentralization came to revolve around the rights of the various minorities. Although the Latvian society did a great deal for the minorities - for instance, nearly twenty per cent of all schools in the mid-1930s were minority schools (Balodis 1990, 217) - there was never a comprehensive legislation passed on the rights of the minority nationalities (von Rauch 1967, 140-41). Rather, there was a tolerance toward the own cultural and educational initiatives and activities of especially the Germans, a tolerance which amounted to a degree of de facto cultural autonomy. On the other hand, one of the stumbling blocks for such a legislation was the German reluctance to regard the Germans as a 'minority nationality' comparable to Russians, Poles and Jews (Garleff 1978, 84).

In sum, none of the two countries had a system of territorial autonomy. There was a degree of cultural decentralization in both, but this did not amount to a recognition of comprehensive organized systems for the administration of ethnically defined cultural autonomy.

Written constitution and minority veto

Both Czechoslovakia and Latvia had written constitutions, and these were precisely the kinds of 'single documents containing the basic rules of governance' that Lijphart writes about (1984, 29). Moreover, both constitutions contained a clear elements of a minority veto as concerns constitutional change. In Czechoslovakia, amendments to the constitution had to be approved by a three-fifths majority in both chambers of the legislature. In Latvia, a two-thirds majority in the saeima was required for such amendments. Moreover, certain fundamental provisions could not be amended without a referendum (Barr Carson 1956, 302-303; Tingsten 1933, 650, 655).

Czechoslovakia and Latvia: conclusions

Czechoslovakia and Latvia were very similar concerning more than half of the dimensions of the Lijphart model. On four of these, they matched Lijphart's characterization of a consensus democracy. They had extreme multiparty systems. These were, moreover, multidimensional in the sense of reflecting several kinds of basic cleavages. Proportional representation was the electoral system in both countries. Also, both Czechoslovakia and Latvia had written constitutions with provisions about minority veto.

Furthermore, both countries *lacked* federal structures and formalized arrangements for nonterritorial autonomy. In both, however, a degree of de facto cultural autonomy was present.

The clearest differences between the two countries were to be found on the remaining three dimensions of the model. Formally, the third of Lijphart's characteristics, bicameralism, would seem to constitute the clearest difference. The Czechoslovak bicameralism - as compared to the unicameral Latvian legislature - was, however, not an example of the kind of *balanced* bicameralism Lijphart presupposes.

As concerns grand coalitions, none of the countries can live up to the requirement of cabinets simultaneously bridging all major societal cleavages. It is, however, clear that Czechoslovakia throughout the interwar period came significantly closer to this than did Latvia. The *Czech* grand coalitions of the first half of the 1920s paved the way for broad coalitions across the ethnic divides in the late 1920s and throughout the 1930s. There remained always some important element of Czechoslovak politics outside the cabinet coalitions - in the late 1930s, the growing separatist sentiment represented by the Henlein and Hlinka parties was this element. Still, the coalitions were broad enough to secure overwhelming parliamentary majorities.

In Latvia, by contrast, Left and Right and even Left and Center remained separated and unable to come together to solve the nation's problems in concert. At the same time, the majorities that the agrarian-led coalitions were able to muster in the saeima were always volatile and offered a feeble basis for at determinate bourgeois democratic action. By way of conclusion, then, it seems that the fact that the socialist-nonsocialist divide was bridged from the very beginning in independent Czechoslovak politics was a precondition of paramount importance for the survivability of democracy in Czechoslovakia.

Of no less importance was the *de facto* separation of powers present in Czechoslovakia but totally absent in Latvia. Masaryk - and as of 1935, Benes - had little formal constitutional power as presidents to determine the course of Czechoslovak politics. The role played by Masaryk before and in connection with the process of Czechoslovak independence made for an immense informal influence as soon as he had been elected to the presidency. The president was the overarching legitimate actor acknowledged by Czechs, Germans and Slovaks. His determination to bring the nationalities together in political cooperation was decisive for the development of democracy in interwar Czechoslovakia. At the same time, the formidable informal power exerted by the Petka in especially questions of economic policy, added to this de facto separation of powers in the country; by its very nature, the Petka was an instrument of political consensus.

In Latvia, by contrast, the presidency never became an alternative source of political power and authority. The country simply lacked a figure of Masaryk's stature who could have become universally recognized as a *pouvoir neutre* by the various parties and groups. In fact, the final showdown leading to the breakdown of democracy was caused by yet another attempt to create a formal separation of powers by increasing the powers of the Latvian president. The Latvian experience shows that a powerful presidency in a segmented society is difficult to achieve unless there are persons with the kind of universal prestige necessary for the job.

In sum, there seem to be crucial differences between the two countries on these last two dimensions. However, it is the informal aspect of these characteristics rather than any formalized arrangements that seem to have made the difference.

Finland and Estonia

There is no better starting point for a general discussion about similarities and differences between Finland and Estonia than the national anthem. The two countries, i.e. Finland and independent Estonia between the world wars as well as today, have the *same* national anthem, known as *Maamme* (Finnish) and *Vårt land* (Swedish) in Finland, and *Mu Isamaa* in Estonia. Clearly, it would seem that sharing a national anthem must mean a great deal of things in common for the two countries.

Nevertheless, the symbolism can be developed even further so as to connote fundamental differences between the countries as well. Metaphorically speaking, then, one might say that the composer means more to the Estonians and the poet whose original text was set to music more to the Finns. Fredrick Pacius, the composer, was German-born; J.L. Runeberg, the poet, was an ethnic Swede living in Finland - he is still considered to be the 'national poet' of the Finns. Estonia's history was molded through a strong German influence from the Middle Ages on. Finland evolved as an integral part of the Swedish kingdom from the 12th Century until 1809; the end of Swedish rule over 'the Eastern Half of the Kingdom' by no means signified an end to Finland's community with Sweden and Scandinavia.

Yet the similarities between the two nations are self-evident as well. The ethnic majorities of the two countries, the Finns and the Estonians, are linguistically related. Even if this affinity is not quite as great as that between, say, Swedish, Norwegian and Danish, it is great enough to be of major practical importance. What is more is that the two nations are, for all practical purposes, each other's *only* kins in a linguistic respect. All other languages belonging to the Finno-Ugric group are either spoken by small groups of people scattered around northern Russia or much too far away from Finnish and Estonian to be of any practical importance (notably Hungarian).

Moreover, their historical development toward independence contains many similarities as well. Estonia came under Russian sovereignty in 1710, Finland in 1809, both as a consequence of the decline of Sweden's role as a European Power. However, the far-reaching autonomy granted to the Finns by the Russian Czar had no equivalent in Estonia.

The period immediately connected with the independence of the both countries constitutes a further similarity. The collapse of the Russian empire was the crucial precondition, and it was in both countries followed by a socialist attempt to seize power. In Finland as well as in Estonia, the revolution attempted by indigenous socialists in concert with Russian bolsheviks was crushed by bourgeois 'freedom fighters' who were to play a significant role in interwar politics in both countries.

As independent states, both countries were dominated by an ethnic majority comprising around ninety per cent of the population. In Finland, practically all of the remaining population was Swedish, whereas there were several ethnic minorities in Estonia. The role of the minorities was, moreover, different in the historical process leading to independence: the Swedes had fought side by side with the Finns to create an independent Finland (and indeed at times led this process), whereas the Estonian minorities lacked a similar role the the process of nation-building.

In terms of party system fragmentation, Finland remained close two European average throughout the interwar period, whereas Estonia was fragmented above this average up until 1932. That year, fragmentation decreased markedly being almost identical with the Finnish level.

In terms of cabinet stability, both countries displayed low values until the early 1930s. From 1932 on, stability increased in Finland, whereas the breakdown of Estonian democracy followed in 1934 subsequent to a couple of years of extremely short-lived cabinets.

Executive power-sharing: grand coalitions

Finland was a divided society after the Civil War of 1918. The idea of a national consensus built on a grand coalition was more or less out of the question; the Left wing, divided though it now was into reformist social democracy and revolutionary communism, was viewed with profound suspicion by the entire nonsocialist camp.

At the same time, the nonsocialist groups and parties who had stood united against the 'reds' in the Civil War (or the War of Freedom, as they preferred to call it), were divided among themselves. Immediately after the war they had been divided into a monarchist and republican camp; the latter emerged victorious as Finland adopted a republican constitution in 1919. The linguistic question, the position of Finnish and Swedish in government and society proved out to be even more divisive.

Throughout the interwar period, Finnish cabinets led an uneasy existence in the cross pressure between the left-right and linguistic dimensions. On several occasions (1920, 1930, 1931) nonsocialist coalitions comprising all major parties including the Swedish People's Party were formed. The two years (1937-39) preceding the Russian attack on Finland saw the establishment of a social democratic-agrarian coalition, which commanded a solid majority in parliament and bridged the divide between socialists and nonsocialists. However, it included no representatives of the Swedish People's Party (Jääskeläinen 1977, 273-610; Karvonen 1989).

The most frequent type of cabinet was a minority cabinet unable to really bridge any of the main cleavages in Finnish politics. Through most of the 1920s, the Swedish Party and the social democrats found themselves in opposition. Although staunchly antisocialist, the former gradually slid into a tacit cooperation with the social democrats, who, unlike Finnish nonsocialist parties, opposed the various 'Finnification' schemes debated in parliament. Since the two parties commanded a majority of the seats they were able to effectively block such initiatives and in fact had considerable leverage over the minority cabinets (Hämäläinen 1966).

All in all, although strengthened and stabilized toward the end of the period, Finnish cabinet politics never experienced anything like a grand coalition in the interwar period.

The *Estonian* case is quite different. Of the seventeen cabinets which ruled between the adoption of the constitution in 1920 and the authoritarian takeover of 1934, only three were minority cabinets. No less than seven were solid majority cabinets commanding sixty or more of the 100 seats in the *Riigikogu*. In 1931 and again in 1932, the two main groups, the socialists and Konstantin Päts' Farmers' Party participated in coalitions together. Both were strong majority cabinets, the latter in fact controlling all of eighty-seven seats in the parliament. For all practical purposes, this was a grand coalition (Mägi 1967, 185-207, 322-323).

Again, however, socialist participation was the exception rather than the rule. Thirteen of the cabinets contained no socialist representation. The typical cabinet was a coalition of centrist or centrist and moderate right wing parties. If the Farmers' Party (moderate right) participated, the cabinet was sure to have a parliamentary majority. Only once (August Rei's cabinet in 1928) did a socialist became Prime Minister; typically enough, the Farmers' Party did not participate in this cabinet (Ibid.; Raun 1987, 113-114).

Majorities, grand coalitions or minority cabinets - the results were pretty much the same. The cabinets lasted a few months, maybe haif a year, and then turned in their resignation. The coalitions seemed to have a remarkably low degree of cohesion and did not bother even to try to maintain a unified façade. Their internal conflicts were there for all to see, and sooner rather than later they brought the cabinet to a fall. Päts' grand coalition of 1932 sat merely around five months, which was in fact somewhat *less* than the life expectancy of an averange Estonian cabinet. It was as if the parties let their conflicts carry over from parliament to cabinet with no moderating element in between.

In sum, none of the countries was characterized by a prevalence of grand coalitions in their executive politics. Finnish cabinets were unable to bridge the two main distinctions - language and left-right - at the same time. In fact many cabinets strictly speaking bridged neither of them effectively. In Estonia, by contrast, majority cabinets were much more common, and de facto grand coalitions occurred a couple of times. At all times, these coalitions remained internally devided and short-lived. There seems to be very little in the way of a correlation between cabinet durability and coalition patterns in the Estonian case.

Separation of powers, formal and informal

The constitution adopted in *Finland* in 1919 created a peculiarly *dualistic* situation in the political life of the country. On the one hand, the parliamentary system based on the radical Representative Reform of 1906 remained in force. The constitution expressedly points to the parliament (*Eduskunta/Riksdag*) as the main exponent of popular sovereignty. At the same time, the 1919 constitution added a strong and real element of presidentialism to the system.

The system as a whole was not based on a clear constitutional doctrine. Quite the contrary, it was a compromise between two competing doctrines, the kind of parliamentary sovereignty that had been established in most other European countries and the president-led executive system of the United States. The compromise reflected the distrust most right-wingers harbored vis-à-vis the parliament; they saw the divisive party politicking between 1907 and 1917 as one of the causes of the chaos which led the nation into a civil war. Moreover, it was a concession toward those who had worked to establish a monarchy in Finland after the Civil War. The separation of powers between the president-led executive branch of government and the legislature was not as clearcut as in the United States. It was, however, real indeed, and in many ways constituted the crucial factor in Finnish politics at large.

The powers of the Finnish president were (and still are) extensive. He appointed the cabinet and the individual ministers. He presided over the cabinet in the Council of State; in this sense, he was the formal initiator of most legislation (bills put to the parliament by the cabinet). He could, moreover, interfere in the legislative process by recalling bills from parliament or by refusing to enact legislation approved by parliament. Moreover he could, basically at any time, dissolve the parliament and call for new elections. Foreign policy leadership was entrusted to the president through the constitution; at the same time, he was the Supreme Commander of the armed forces. Finally, he had extensive appointive powers concerning the highest echelons of state administration (Kastari 1969; Nousiainen 1971).

All the same, the parliamentary mechanism gave the legislature some not inconsiderable checks on the president's powers. Foremost of them was the fundamental principle of parliamentarism: that the cabinet and its ministers have the confidence of the majority of the parliament. At any time, parliament could vote the cabinet or an individual minister out of office through a vote of non-confidence. Thus, the president in practice had to consider the prevailing opinions in parliament when appointing cabinets and ministers. Moreover, parliament could overrule the presidential veto against legislation by approving it anew after elections (Ibid.).

Finland had, in a word, a parliamentary and presidential system all at once. It went as as far in the direction of presidentialism as was possible without undermining the fundamental principle of parliamentarism. The separation of powers was not as clearcut as in the American case. Still, Finland was one of the prime examples of a separation of governmental powers among European democracies.

Estonia was in this respect at the opposite extreme. In few, if any, countries was the sovereignty of the parliament so thoroughly carried out as in Estonia. There was no president at all in the formal sense. Instead, the Eldest of the State (*Riigivanem*) performed the representative functions of a Head of State, while at the same time presiding over the plenary meetings of the cabinet as prime minister. The cabinet, the *Riigivanem* as well as the individual ministers, were appointed by the parliament on the basis of a proposal by its Speaker (Mägi 1967, 163-163). The cabinet and its leader could at any time be removed from office by a vote of nonconfidence by the legislature. Even the Supreme Court judges were elected by parliament (Raun 1967, 113). To the extent that there was a check on the powers of the legislature it was not to be excercised by the executive but through a mechanism of direct democracy. If 25,000 voters thus demanded, an issue could be put to a referendum or a popular initiative for legislation could be presented. A slow and elaborate channel for political decisions, referenda and popular initiatives remained all but a dead letter in Estonian constitutional life throughout the 1920s. The crisis of the early thirties stirred renewed interest in direct democracy. After repeated attempts, a 1933 referendum finally gave the executive branch of government decsively enlarged powers. The political crisis had, however, proceeded so far that this reform turned out to have come too late (Parming 1975, 41-44).

The differences between Finland and Estonia concerning the separation of governmental powers are as clear as one can possibly imagine in the case of two parliamentary democracies. The importance of these dissimilarities becomes all the more evident when one surveys the course of the political crisis in both countries. The early 1930s witnessed somewhat of a showdown between the government and the extreme right in Finland as well as in Estonia; in both cases, the role of the civil war veterans and their followers was crucial.

From the late fall of 1929 onward, the Lapua Movement at times constituted the most important actor in Finnish politics. Originally a comprehensive anti-communist movement, it gradually took on an increasingly clear antidemocratic, even outright fascist character. It was initially met with sympathy and concessions on the part of the government; its increasingly violent character led the government to gradually withdraw its support and start finding ways to limit Lapua's influence. In February, 1932, it finally came to a direct confrontation between the Lapua Movement and the government.

Unlike many other extreme right-wing movements in Europe, Lapua had not created a military organization of its own. This would have constituted a challenge against the Civil Guards, a militia system based on the victorious White Army of the Civil War of 1918. The Civil Guards commanded something like a hundred thousand men (as compared to the 30, 000 troops of the regular defense forces). They were largely financed through government appropriations and integrated into the defense system of the Republic.

Lapua counted on the fidelity of the Civil Guards in critical instances. However, the Civil Guards were not - just as the White Army of 1918 had not been - made up of right wing people only. Centrist and agrarian sympathisers were in large numbers active in them as well, and liberal and agrarian politicians saw to it that the Guards were kept formally non-political. As Lapua in 1932 called upon the Guards to to oppose the government, the Guards started to mobilize, but many did this under considerable bewilderment.

President P. E. Svinhufvud, long sympathetic to the Lapua
Movement and in fact brought to power largely thanks to Lapua, finally made up his mind and turned against the movement. This was to prove decisive as to the opinions within the Civil Guards (Alapuro 1988, 209-214). He went on national radio and told the Guards to refrain from any unlawful actions and simply to return home in good order. 'This I order as the Supreme

Commander of the Civil Guards'.

The last formulation is surely not without significance. Most of the units were led by professional officers on the payroll of the regular armed forces. In the confused situation that the process of a de facto attempt at a coup d'etat had created, these were words any professional soldier understood: a Superior issues a command, the men obey. And the president *was* their superior, as he was Supreme Commander of the armed forces, including the Civil Guard system. In this critical situation, Svinhufvud did not have to rely on political persuasion only; the presidency furnished him with a purely military authority as well (Karvonen 1991 B, 106-115).

The situation was entirely different in Estonia. The Civil War Veterans *were* the extreme right-wing movement. They were not only openly political and in fact increasingly fascist; they were also the chief rivals of the established parties and politicians, including Päts. Far from being formally subordinate to the government, they viewed the governmental system and the political actors with profound suspicion. It was the Veterans who were the chief engine behind the demands of a radically strengthened executive power; this they finally achieved through the referendum of October, 1933. Having forced through a strong presidency they declared that General Andres Larka was their presidential candidate. As it was evident that he had more than a real chance of being popularly elected, Päts, in fact supported by the entire party field, carried out his bloodless coup in March, 1934 (Parming 1975, 41-46; Raun 1987, 115-120).

The above account may seem like a long excursion from the simple factual description of the separation of governmental powers in the two countries. However, it vividly illustrates the way in which formal powers may work in critical situations. The separation of powers in Finland not just made for a generally strong executive. It made for a balance of sorts in the political life at large, as the president enjoyed the support of many right-wingers that looked upon the parliament and the cabinet with disdain. In Estonia, the gap between the government and the 'disloyal opposition' was much more clearcut, while at the same time the executive was extremely weak. In sum, it seems that the separation of powers is a crucial factor explaining the different outcomes of interwar politics in the Finnish and Estonian cases.

Balanced bicameralism and minority representation

This section must of necessity be extremely short. Both Finland and Estonia had unicameral legislatures, and the elections to the parliaments contained no special provisions to ensure minority representation. The Finnish legislature received its structure as early as 1906, as the radical - indeed pathbreaking, as compared to the rest of Europe - Representative Reform was carried out. It is sometimes suggested that the Grand Committee of the Finnish parliament could function as something of a second chamber, invested as it is with the authority of an overall scrutiny of legislative bills. Most analyses have revealed, however, that the Grand Committee is more of a 'register office than a chamber' (Helander 1976).

Similarly, the 1920 Estonian constitution provided for a unicameral legislature. There were no moderating elements to this unicameralism in the organization of the parliament. Nor was there a mechanism connected to the election of the members of the *Riigikogu* which would have secured a given representation for any minority (Mägi 1967, 135-183).

The party system: parties and dimensions

Again, these are two countries with marked multiparty systems. There were 6-8 parties represented in the Finnish parliament during the interwar period, whereas the number of parties in the Estonian legislature ranged from six to fourteen. The consolidation of the Estonian party system prior to Päts' takeover meant that there were in fact fewer parties in Estonia than in Finland around 1933.

There were both considerable similarities and important differences in the cleavages structuring the party systems of the two countries. The Left-Right dimension was salient, but being markedly rural societies, both countries also had strong and influential agrarian parties. Moreover, there was an ethnic dimension in the party system, as national minorities in both countries had party organizations of their own.

The Left was in both countries divided into a larger reformist party and a smaller de facto communist party. The position of the Estonian communists was undermined over time; by 1932, they only had five seats in parliament, having commanded ten seats a decade earlier. In Finland, the communists were wiped out in 1930 through the anti-communist legislation forced upon the parliament by the Lapua Movement. Before that, they had mustered a little over a third of the Left vote. All in all, the Left wing was consistently somewhat stronger in Finland than in Estonia. The Estonian Left never controlled more than 34 of the 100 parliamentary seats, and by 1932 this figure was down to 27. In Finland, by contrast, social democracy, unrivaled on the Left, grew throughout the 1930s. By 1939 it had all of 85 seats (42.5 per cent) in parliament.

The two dominant agrarian parties, the Finnish Agrarian Union and the Estonian Farmers' Party, were of roughly equal size (around one-fourth of the parliamentary seats) throughout the 1920s). Before the 1932 elections, however, the Estonian party merged with (or swallowed) several of the smaller centrist and right-wing parties, becoming the United Aagrarian Party. The election gave the new party no less than 42 seats. Besides this not inconsiderable difference in size after 1932, there was a notable difference between the Finnish and the Estonian parties throughout the period as concerns their general ideological posture. Although largely a catch-all party for the farming population, the Finnish Agrarian Union was clearly a centrist party. Some of its policies concerning social and economic matters were in fact fairly radical (which eventually helped the agrarians to find a common platform with the social democrats). The Estonian Farmers' Party, by contrast, was more clearly a conservative party. Therefore, it was also supported by the numerically limited but socially influential Estonian upper class mainly residing in the cities (Parming 1975, 18). The Finnish conservative vote, by contrast, was controlled by the National Coalition Party (and the Swedish People's Party as concerns the Swedish voters). A difference between Finland and Estonia was in fact that there was a fairly large independent (not primarily agrarian) conservative party in the former but not in the latter.

The ethnic cleavage was more important and more straightforward in Finnish than in Estonian politics. The only ethnic party in Finland was the Swedish People's Party. Although it never commanded more than approximately twelve per cent of the seats in parliament, it carried considerable influence and participated in several cabinets. In cooperation with the Left, particularly the social democrats who also fought attempts at curbing bilingualism, the Swedish party managed to fend off most of the attacks from Finnish nationalists.

Estonia, by contrast, had three different ethnic parties - a Russian, a German and a minuscule Swedish party - the latter two of which united in an electoral alliance in 1929. The representation of the ethnic parties peaked in 1932, when their the seats totaled eight.

Finally, the electorally weak position of liberalism and the absence of regionalism apart from the ethnic dimension are features typical of the party systems of Finland as well as Estonia (von Rauch 174, 91-97).

All in all, the party systems and cleavage structures of the two countries are relatively similar: both had typical multiparty systems based on multiple politically relevant dimensions.

Proportional representation

Again, both countries match the Lijphart model in that they had typical proportional voting systems. The elections to the *Finnish* parliament were based on the d'Hondt version of the highest average system. The details of this well-known electoral system need not be accounted for here (see, e.g., Mackie and Rose 1991, 505-506). Suffice it to say that the Finnish version of PR slightly favored large parties. This however, by no means hindered small parties from entering parliament; in 1933, for instance, there were five parties that had less than ten per cent of the seats each.

The *Estonian* electoral system was extremely proportional. This was particularly a consequence of the fact that - for all practical purposes - the entire country formed a single electoral district. Thus, according to Mägi, merely one per cent of the vote (less that five thousand votes) was enough to secure a parliamentary seat in the early 1920s. In the 1923 election, twenty-six parties ran for parliament; as many as fourteen of them gained seats. In 1926, proportionality was restricted so that a party, in order to be represented in the *Riigikogu* must have gained a minimum of two seats. This gradually brought down the number of parties to a certain extent. Still, the degree of proportionality in the voting system remained high (Mägi 1967, 175-176).

Territorial and nonterritorial federalism and decentralization

Finland is a unitary state. In fact is lacks an intermediate or regional political organization typical of not just federal states but also of many nonfederal systems. The provincial or county administration (Finnish *lääni*, Swedish *län*) is a regional intrument of the central government; it contains no elective offices.

What there is of decentralization - over and above the highly developed powers of local governments - is related to the linguistic question. The formally most clearcut example of territorial decentralization is the autonomous status of Aaland Islands. This large group of skerries centered around a larger main island in the Swedish-speaking archipelago in the extreme Southwest was granted extensive autonomy after a conflict which had ensued from the Aalanders' attempt to reunite their region with Sweden in 1918. The conflict was resolved by the League of Nations in the favor of Finland on the condition that Finland grant an autonomous status to Aaland.

Apart from this single exception - which after all, concerned only some twenty thousand people - there were no examples of territorial federalism in Finland. However, the cultural needs of the Swedish population did give rise to important forms of nonterritorial decentralization. Thus, a Swedish diocese was created to administer the Swedish congregations within the established Lutheran church. A Swedish division in the National Board of Education similarly heads the Swedish school system. Moreover, *Nylands Brigad* has the main responsibility for the military training of the Swedish conscripts in Finland.

Similarly a unitarian state, *Estonia* also witnessed the establishment of a degree of cultural autonomy for its minorities. Although they had declared their intentions to grant the minorities such autonomous rights in connection with the creation of the constitution, the Estonian leaders were hesitant to let this principle be put into practice in the early 1920s. Their attitude changed after the communist attempt at coup d'etat in 1924; the German role in crushing this attempt was central. The goodwill this created forced the government to finally give the long envisaged cultural autonomy of the minorities legal status in February, 1925. It was particularly important to the

Germans, who lived scattered around Estonia, to create an administrative structure to manage their cultural activities. The Cultural Council of the Estonian Germans became that main instrument. The Russians and the Swedes, by contrast, could largely manage their cultural affairs within the framework of the local self-government (Weiss 1967, 169-174).

In sum, both countries display examples of nonterritorial decentralization. The status of the Aaland Islands in Finland is the sole example of outright territorial autonomy. Generally speaking, the decentralist arrangements in Finland were more extensive and concerned a considerably larger number of citizens than in Estonia. Also, the constitutionally different status of the Swedes in Finland - they are not a minority but one of the two indigenous nationalities - should be borne in mind.

Written constitution and minority veto

The *Finnish* Constitution Act of 1919 is a detailed document of paramount importance to the concrete functioning of the political system. However, it is, strictly speaking, not *the* Finnish Constitution. In order for the interwar constitutional framework to be complete, the Parliament Act, the Ministerial Liability Act and the Chancellor of Justice and the High Court of Impeachment Act must also be mentioned. These documents taken together formed the constitutional framework of interwar politics in Finland. In fact, the tension inherent in the constitutional dualism in the Finnish system has kept the role of the constitution central throughout the period of Finnish independence. It was not until the early 1990s that careful amendments to the constitution started to appear.

One of the politically most powerful provisions in the Finnish constitution concerned   the requirements for qualified majorities. Changes in the constitution and *other laws which must be passed in a constitutional order* - and these latter cases were much more numerous than in most comparable systems - required the backing of substantial majority in parliament. They could either be passed by a two-thirds majority and, after elections, a renewed two-thirds majority in the newly elected parliament, or if they were declared to be urgent, by a single five-sixths majority. These were heavy requirements, and they placed considerable pressures toward consensus among the parties in parliament. At the same time, they granted relatively small minorities - in the latter case, merely 34 MPs - a powerful veto (Anckar 1990, 35-36).

Estonia had a single written constitution containing provisions for all main features of the country's political system. Unlike Finland, however, the restrictions to the legislative powers of the parliament were not placed inside the *Riigikogu* itself in the form of far-reaching a minority veto. Rather, the Estonian constitution contained (as was noted above) a considerable element of direct democracy. Constitutional amendments always had to be approved by the majority of the people in a referendum. Thus, where the Finnish constitution gave parliamentary minorities special privileges, the Estonian system sought an alternative platform by placing considerable powers directly in the hands of the people (Mägi 1967, 246-257)

In sum, both countries had detailed written constitutions. The Finnish constitution was not, however, a single written document. Finland had, moreover, procedures which guaranteed a more effective minority veto in legislative matters than what was the case in Estonia.

Finland and Estonia: conclusions

Finland and Estonia scored similarly on most of the dimensions of the Lijphart model. Both lacked the balanced bicameralism presupposed by consensus democracy; in fact they had quite orthodox unicameral legislative systems. They had multiparty systems based on multiple social cleavages. Proportional voting systems existed in both countries; in Estonia, the degree of proportionality in the electoral system was extremely high. Moreover, they were both unitary states, but the cultural and social needs of the linguistic minorities had given rise to a degree of nonterritorial (and in the case of Aaland, also territorial) decentralization. Finally, they both had specific written constitutions.

As for differences, there was a higher degree of minority parliamentarism in Finland than in Estonia. Most Estonian cabinets had (at least in the formal sense) the backing of the parliamentary majority, but this did not seem to render them any more stable than the minority cabinets. In fact, Estonia unlike

Finland had a couple of de facto grand coalitions; the durability of these cabinets was, however, no more impressive than that of the others. In Finland the clear majority of the cabinets were minority cabinets. A more stable pattern of majority cabinets was only established through the 'red-green' compromise of 1937. Nevertheless, Finland never saw a true grand coalition uniting the social democrats, the agrarians and the Swedish People's Party, a coalition that would have bridged the socialist-nonsocialist distinction and the linguistic cleavage at the same time.

The Estonian system lacked the effective minority veto required for a wide spectrum of 'constitutional legislation' in Finland. These checks on the legislative powers of the parliamentary majority lie in the hands of the people through the provisions for referenda in the case of constitutional revisions. Because of the narrower scope of legislation comprised by these provisions and due to the practical difficulties connected with arranging a referendum, these provisions did not become an effective instrument in Estonian politics. By contrast, the extensive Finnish minority veto constantly forced the parliament to arrive at a consensus in order to be able to pass legislation.

Most significantly, however, the Finnish system contained an effective separation of powers totally absent in Estonia. The powers of the Finnish president made it possible for him to not only exert extensive influence on the central political institutions. He could also control the armed forces, including the Civil Guard system. As was demonstrated above this made it possible for him to resolve the acute crisis of 1932. He invoked his powers as the Supreme Commander of the Civil Guards in a situation where the prestige of the parliamentary system was completely insufficient to persuade the Guards to toe the line.

In sum, both countries share several features typical of consociational democracies according to Lijphart. At the same time, they are both some distance away from the ideal model. Despite the similarities between Finland and Estonia there is at least one crucial difference which seems to go a long way toward explaining the outcome of the interwar crisis.

France and Austria

From the point of view of fragmentation theory, this is certainly the most troublesome of the three pairs of countries surveyed in this chapter. The French party system was highly fragmented (Rae's F ranging from 0.75 to 0.84), cabinet stability was low, but democracy weathered the interwar crisis. Austria, by contrast, had a highly concentrated party system (F between 0.59 and 0.66): nevertheless, cabinet duration remained low, and democracy finally broke down in 1933. This pair of countries simply defies the logic of fragmentation theory altogether; it is inconceivable that the two countries should score similarly on one dimension (cabinet instability) as they are far apart concerning party system fragmentation and the 'final outcome' is different.

In many other respects as well, Austria and France seem far apart. France's republican traditions dating back to the Revolution are contrasted with the monarchical and imperial past to which only the defeat in the World War put a rather abrupt end. The outcome of the war was, of course, in itself a major difference. Austria belonged to the group of defeated nations, France was one of the victors. Consequently, France between the world wars was one of the 'old states' with borders secured over long periods of time. Austria was a 'rump state' built on the main parts of the German-speaking lands of the former Double Monarchy.

Ethno-linguistically, Austria after World War I was one of the most homogeneous states in Europe. Only a couple of per cent of the population spoke languages other than German. The change from the multilingual situation characteristic of the Habsburg Empire was, therefore, dramatic. France also was fairly homogeneous: something like ninety-three per cent of the population were French-speakers (the regional variation was, to be sure, considerable; the dominant variety of French originally spoken in the area around Paris was a 'second language' for many citizens regarded as 'French-speaking). Among the linguistic minorities proper, Alsatian Germans and Bretons were the largest groups. All in all, Austria and France approach the homogeneous rather than multi-ethnic end of the continuum (Rundle 1946, 67, 81-82).

In sum, these countries form a pair of comparison which is quite different from the two pairs discussed above. Consequently, the explanatory power of the consensus model is put to a different test in this comparative case study.

Executive power-sharing: grand coalitions

Unlike all our other cases, the immediate postwar era entailed no profound change in *French* politics. The laws passed in 1875 continued to form the legal and constitutional framework of political life, and the party system, fluid as it was, largely reflected tendencies familiar from the earlier decades of the Third Republic. Much of what was true of French politics before the World War applies to the interwar period as well.

Although new types of government coalitions certainly appeared in the course of the years between the world wars, the functioning of the system and the complications typical of executive power-sharing were largely the same as in earlier years. Parties were difficult to define, which is why parliamentary groups were difficult to define; and since the borders between various groups in parliament were difficult to determine, the parliamentary base of executive coalitions at all times remained somewhat uncertain. French coalition politics was a constant process of negotiation inside the coalitions as well as in the National Assembly, not just between parties but between individual ministers and parliamentary deputies as well (Adamthwaite 1977,9; Dogan 1989, 243-246). Except for the socialist (SFIO) and communist (PCF) parties, many authors have preferred to speak about *tendances* rather than organized parties. The argument could be carried even further: the electorate consisted of tendances rather than party constituencies, the parliamentary groups consisted of tendances rather than party caucuses, and executive coalitions of tendances rather than blocs clearly defined in terms of partisan bases.

Hazy as they were, the cabinet coalitions were very much at the center of French politics. Over time, the tendances behind them shifted enough to enable us to speak of rightist, centrist and leftist coalition periods. Whether a coalition had a majority or minority status is really not a meaningful question. Initially, cabinets normally had the parliamentary majority behind them; equally routinely, however, this support started to fade before too long. Nevertheless, this much is clear: grand coalitions were not the rule in interwar French politics.

Georges Clemenceau's abortive quest for the presidency (he had been Prime Minister between 1917 and 1920) was followed by a series of cabinets leaning toward the right wing. These cabinets were mainly based on the *Bloc National*, the numerous rightist and right-of-center parties. Although situated to the left of this bloc, the *Gauche Radicale* as well as the Republican Socialists frequently joined it in forming cabinets; in fact the support of the former was the normal requirement for parliamentary majorities in interwar French politics. In connection with the 1924 elections, however, the Radical Left, now in deep disagreement with the National Bloc over foreign policy as well as financial issues, formed an electoral alliance with the Socialist Party. A precondition for this cartel was the rift between socialists and communists, which had occurred in 1920. After a victory for *Cartel des Gauches* in the election, a series of 'center-left' cabinets followed. The radicals occupied most ministerial posts in the cabinets, the socialists provided the necessary numbers in parliament; the socialists had doctrinal doubts about participating in governments themselves. Two years later, however, the financial crisis still looming large, this cabinet pattern had reached the end of the tether. Raymond Poincaré then went on to form a broad *'cabinet of national unity'* backed by all parties to the right of the Socialist Party. Poincaré remained the central figure in French cabinet politics up until 1929, when he left political life due to ill health. Nevertheless, he had led French politics during a period of relative executive stability; the parties of Center and Right had guaranteed him a substantial parliamentary majority (Thomson 1969, 150-151; Greene 1970, 32-44; McMillan 1985, 88-94; Rémond 1969, 254-273).

An interregnum of rapidly shifting coalitions followed upon Poincaré's departure from politics. The instability was greatly acerbated by the onset of the Great Depression. After the violent clashes of february 6, 1934, where an extreme right wing takeover seemed a distinct possibility (Greene 1970, 65-70), the Radical Left, the socialists and the communists proclaimed a *Popular Front* against fascism. Referring to the Dreyfus Affair, Jackson (1988, 3) writes that the Left again had resorted to its 'traditional response to any threat against the Republic...unity'.

Having won a great victory in the 1936 election the socialists for the first time entered the cabinet, taking office togther with the radicals. This Popular Front cabinet headed by Léon Blum initially had the backing of the communists as well. This relationship was soon strained and the communists withdrew their support (Tiersky 1974, 83-95). At the same time, a polarization took place across the entire party field. When Blum's second cabinet was eventually replaced by Daladier's cabinet in 1938, this marked a very clear shift to the right. The *Gauche Radicale*, once again a pivotal party, had slid considerably to the right and denounced the Popular Front. The period immediately prior to the outbreak of the war was marked by increasing ideological entrenchment also among those parties which were normally regarded as democratic parties in France (McMillan 1985, 114-115; Greene 1970, 80-112).

Executive power-sharing there certainly was, but real grand coalitions did not occur in France between the World Wars. The *Gauche Radicale*, less and less radical over the years, remained the perennial cabinet participant in periods of centrist, rightist as well as leftist rule. The most encompassing cabinet model was that of 'national unity', which only excluded the socialist parties proper.

Austrian cabinet coalitions, transient as they also normally were, were based on a much more rigid pattern of support and opposition. In fact, what was distinctly absent from Austrian politics was any real alternation in power. This goes to say that not only were grand coalitions absent throughout the period; what there were of shifts in cabinet composition concerned the margins rather than the center stage of Austrian politics.

The relative immobility of Austrian coalition patterns from 1920 to 1934 is all the more striking in view of the fact that the transition to the republican form of government was carried out by cabinets that were indeed grand coalitions. The 'revolutionary ministry' of 1918 included Christian social, German nationalist as well as social democratic ministers. It was followed by coalitions of Christian socials and social democrats. These were no narrow cabinets; the combined shares of the two parties amounted to almost eighty per cent of the vote. As soon as the Constitution had been passed (October, 1920), however, the coalition fell apart. The coalition pattern that was to follow after the the constitutional settlement stood in a stark contrast to the grand coalitions of the transitional period.

The most striking feature of Austrian executive politics was the role of the social democrats as the permanent opposition. Not once after the transitional period did the social democrats enter a cabinet. Only once were they more or less forced to cooperate with the Christian socials on a major issue in parliament. This was the question of the 1929 constitutional reform (see next section); it did not manifest itself at the cabinet level in the form of a coalition (Hoor 1966, 99-103).

The center of gravity of Austrian cabinets was at all times the Christian Social Party. With more than forty per cent of the seats in the *Nationalrat*, it achieved parliamentary majorities with the help of the other nonsocialist groups. Throughout the 1920s, coalitions made up of the Christian socials and the Greater German People's Party (*Grossdeutsche Volkspartei*) reigned. The relations between the two parties became increasingly strained, however, and from 1932 on the Greater Germans no longer participated in government. Instead, the more or less clearly fascist *Heimwehr* movement and its party arm *Heimatblock*, as well as the conservative Peasant League (*Landbund*) provided the cabinets with the necessary majority. When *Landbund* withdrew its support in May, 1933, the cabinet under Engelbert Dollfuss was already taking decisive steps toward a dictatorship (Hoor 1966, 99-105; Kitchen 1980, 173-199; Tingsten 1936, 195-204).

In sum, none of the countries saw an establishment of a grand coalition in the interwar period (the transitional years in Austria are not considered as part of the interwar period). As to alternation in executive power, the French system displayed a clearly greater degree of flexibility than the Austrian pattern of cabinets. The immobility of the Austrian cabinet constellations contrasted with the shifts from right to left - always with the radicals as the moderating force - in French politics.

Separation of powers, formal and informal

The constitutional laws passed in *France* in 1875 provided for a parliamentary system as well as for a president with not inconsiderable independent powers. According to the constitution, he appointed the ministers of the cabinet and higher government officials. Moreover, he supervised the armed forces and had the power to conclude treaties with foreign powers. On the other hand, he was elected through a joint vote in the two chambers of the National Assembly, a feature which underlined the central position of the legislature in the French constitutional system. Still, the constitution granted the president some checks on parliamentary power. Among these, the power of dissolution (with the consent of the Senate, the upper house) and the right to send back legislation to the assembly for 'reconsideration' were foremost (Thomson 1969, 75-101; Hermens 1958, 265-266; Tingsten 1933, 128-129).

In practice, the powers of the president were dramatically reduced in the course of the Third Republic years (Duverger 1968, 455). A series of 'presidential crises'- the first in 1877 and the last in 1924 - stripped the president of his main powers. The power of dissolution became a dead letter, and the president was not expected to express a will independent of that of the parliamentary majority in connection with cabinet formations and executive crises. Thus, as Thomson writes (1969, 96)

> With the decline in importance of the President, the executive power concentrated completely in the hands of the cabinet, under the *Président du Cabinet*, which in turn depended for its existence and survival entirely on the support of a majority of the Chamber.

This extremely parliament-centered view of the Third Republic is naturally largely accurate. It is still probable that it has tended to be somewhat caricatured in much of the literature. A keen contemporary observer, Herbert Tingsten notes that the informal influence of the president was often considerable (1933, 212-213). Moreover, he points to a factor overlooked by most other authors; the powers of the *cabinet* itself. In a comparative European perspective, the powers of the French cabinet were quite formidable. Its farreaching decree powers and its control of the centralized state bureaucracy in combination with the fact that much of French legislation consisted of principal rules rather than detailed statutes placed a great deal of de facto power in the hands of the ministers. In conjunction with the high degree of personal continuity among the executive elite, this made for cabinets which, while certainly being sensitive to parliamentary moods, could in critical situations act surprisingly effectively. French executive politics was complicated by the predominance of the multiparty parliament; it was, however, not paralyzed by it or completely subjugated to it (Tingsten 1933, 215).

The *Austrian* constitution of 1920 created a clearly parliament-centered system. The powers were to lie with the bicameral legislature. The parliament appointed the Federal President for a four-year period, it picked the ministers of the cabinet including its leader, the Federal Chancellor, and it appointed the judges of the Federal Constitutional Court. The powers of the president were largely decorative; he could neither dissolve the parliament nor decide upon cabinet formations or dismissals. It had been the social democrats who particularly feared a strong presidency; they had resisted attempts at direct popular election of the president and at granting him substantial independent powers (Gulick 1948, 107-108; Graham 1924, 166-181).

Throughout the 1920s, rightist groups argued for a strengthened executive power as a means to greater political stability in Austria. Towards the end of the decade, when violent clashes between *Heimwehr* and social democratic *Schutzbunds* had started to occur, the Social Democratic Party was gradually forced to adopt a more conciliatory position in the question of constitutional reform. The main reason was that the social democrats feared a fascist takeover in case an agreement between the political camps did not take place. Having fended off many of the proposals advanced by the Christian socials - including, i.a., a de facto semi-corporatist representation - the social democrats agreed on a major revision of the constitution in 1929. According to these changes, the president would be elected by a direct popular vote for a period of six years. He was given appointive powers as concerns the members of the cabinet and the power to dissolve parliament. The members of the Constitutional Court could be dismissed, and new members appointed by the president. The cabinet was granted extraordinary legislative and budgetary powers. All in all, the reform entailed severe reductions in the powers of the parliament and, consequently, in the potential influence of the social democrats (Hoor 1966, 102; Gulick 1948, 775-880).

However, the effects of the reform remained limited. The president was never elected by the people. Instead, incumbent Wilhelm Miklas was chosen by the parliament anew. More significantly, the presidential power to dissolve the parliament and call for new elections was not utilized, although several instances of total deadlock occurred. Wilhelm Miklas clearly manifested his loyalty to the democratic constitution and tried to persuade Dollfuss informally to give up his course apparently headed toward dictatorship. Dollfuss was, however, backed by *Heimwehr* which no longer pretended to be anything else than it had always been: a fascist movement intent on crushing democracy.

Shortly after the constitutional revision *Heimwehr,* who had been among the loudest actors demanding a revision, proclaimed its Korneuburg Program denouncing democracy wholesale. Apparently, Miklas simply did not believe that his formal powers would be effective in stopping the antidemocratic course chosen by the dollfussian wing of Christian socials backed by the outright fascist movement. With the benefit of hindsight it seems that the constitutional revision - if it could ever have been a remedy to Austria's political problems - had come too late; for many of the groups and politicians who had demanded it, it primarily seems to have been an instrument to crush the social democrats (Andics 1984, 170-184; Hoor 1966, 102-103; Tingsten 1936, 195-204).

Conclusions concerning the separation of powers in interwar France and Austria are not simple. On the one hand, France had had a degree of presidentialism which had largely disappeared before the period began. On the other hand, Austria introduced a strong and independent executive a few years before democracy broke down; these powers, however, were not used effectively during the remaining years of Austrian democracy. Moreover, French politics contained some informal mechanisms which to a certain extent strengthened the indepenet room to meneuver of the executive. All in all, however, it is correct to say that both systems were quite parliament-centered.

Balanced bicameralism and minority representation

The way the constitutional laws of 1875 were written, it is obvious that a balanced bicameral legislature was what the founding fathers of the *French* Third Republic had intended to create. The Chamber of Deputies was to reflect the democratic principle and be elected every four years by popular vote based on universal suffrage. The Senate, on the other hand, was to be a conservative factor which would balance the supposed democratic radicalism of the Chamber. A third of its members were be elected triannually for a nine-year period (the original two-thirds were appointed for life by the National Assembly). The elections were indirect; the final choice of senators was made by an electoral college made up of representatives for regional and communal councils. This made for a clear overrepresentation of the countryside; the small rural communes were particularly favored. The two Chambers of the National Assembly had basically identical constitutional powers (Hermens 1958, 265-267; Thomson 1969, 93-94; Duverger 1968, 454-455).

However, due to pressures from the Republican wing of early Third Republic politics, the electoral basis of the Senate was changed as early as 1884. This reform gave the larger communes greatly increased weight in the electoral colleges by grading representation according to the size of the municipal council, which in turn was relative to the size of the population in a commune. In practice, this meant that the representative pattern in the Senate became more similar to that of the Chamber. However, the two chambers were still far from identical: the 'overrepresentation' of the countryside in the Senate continued to be clear even after the Reform (Thomson 1969, 95).

Moreover, the fact that financial bills were to be handled first in the Chamber before they reached the Senate (which had the power to amend or reject the decisions of the Chamber) over time shifted the center of gravity of French politics to the Chamber. It was in connection with the negotiations in the Chamber that crucial deals were struck, and the Senate seldom made major changes in financial decisions taken by the Chamber. With the simultaneous decline of the president's role the relative position of the Chamber as compared to the Senate was strengthened further (Tingsten 1933, 130-131; Thomson 1969, 95-96; Hermens 1958, 265-267).

These changes notwithstanding, it is fair to say that France had a relatively balanced two-chamber system which provided for minority (regional) representation as well.

The social democrats managed to fend off a strong Upper House in the *Austrian* constitutional system. The nonsocialist parties had advocated a powerful *Bundesrat* based on equal representation for the regions, including the city of Vienna. This would have severely limited the influence of the Social Democratic Party which almost completely depended on Vienna for support. Instead of balanced bicameralism, a two-chamber system clearly emphasizing the *Nationalrat* was created. This Lower House of parliament was to be elected through direct popular vote based on universal suffrage, whereas the members of the upper house were chosen by the Territorial Diets. No region was to have less than three or more than twelve members in the *Bundesrat*.

The center of legislative power lie clearly in the lower house. The upper house had a suspensive veto over normal legislative bills; this veto could, however, be overruled by the *Nationalrat* through repassage of the law by an absolute majority. Moreover, the *Bundesrat*s power of veto did not encompass money bills or bills that concerned the rules of procedure in the lower house or aimed at dissolving it (Gulick 1948, 106-108; Graham 1924, 167-169).

Throughout the 1920s, the *Nationalrat* was the power center of Austrian politics. In connection with the 1929 constitutional revision, however, the *Bundesrat* was formally replaced by a de facto corporatist chamber - this reflected the wishes of *Heimwehr* in particular. However, thanks to a a juridic trick this amendment was never enacted, which is why the two houses continued their work in the same way as before (Gulick 1948, 876-877).

In sum, both France and Austria had bicameral legislatures. The role of the lower house was dominant in both countries. It is clear, nevertheless, that France came closer to Lijphart's 'balanced bicameralism' than Austria.

Parties and dimensions

The party systems of the two countries add to the paradoxical image presented by this comparative case study in many other respects. France had really just one dominant dimension that separated the parties, but the number of parties was high. The Austrian party system was structured according to several salient dimensions, but there were few parties.

It is of course an exaggeration to call the *French* party system purely one-dimensional. In fact the multitude of parties naturally reflected a great number of important issues on which the parties differed to a certain extent. As an organizing principle, as a criterion for how the parties related to each other, however, the left-right scale was clearly more important than other cleavages. True, there were parties which were close to the catholic church and others that stood for anticlerical traditions. There were parties on the Right in which monarchistic tendencies were still visible. There were parties that largely depended on certain regions and had little or no support in others. Still, the final battle over republic contra monarchy had been fought in connection with the Dreyfus Affair; the laicist principles codified as laws were unpopular among certain nonsocialist parties but they were firmly established; parties had their clear regional strongholds but regionalism as an overarching dimension meant little. All parties except the 'bolshevized' communists were nationalistic; nationalism was a matter of degree rather than dispute (Thomson 1969, 103-110; Tiersky 1974, 23-53).

So the existing parties were in many ways reflections of a cleavage structure which had become obsolete. As parties, quite like other organizations, do not wish to put themselves out of business, they continued their activities, well anchored in clientelist and personalist practices in regional and local contexts. Depending on the point in time and the way of counting, there were three rightist or conservative parties, the largest of them being *Union républicaine démocratique*. Centrist and liberal parties numbered four or five, notably *Républicains de gauche*. The 'Left', finally, more and more diversified over the years, consisted of five different groups (the communists were not regarded as part of the *'gauche'* of French politics). We have already noted the pivotal role of *Gauche Radicale*, but this was not the largest of these parties. The Republican Radicals/Radical Socialists and the French Socialist Party formed the largest bloc, mustering around one-sixth of the seats each (Mackie and Rose 1991, Table 7.3c; Thomson 1969, 103-110; Tingsten 1933, 205-207; Hermens 1958, 267-269).

In *Austria*, the left-right dimension was certainly also the most important cleavage separating the parties. All the same, both clericalism and nationalism were important dimensions structuring the party system and profoundly affecting their relationships with each other. The concept of 'camps' (*Lager*) in Austrian politics is based on the salience of these dimensions (Botz 1980, 195-199).

The socialist and therefore anticlerical social democrats ruled in a sovereign manner in 'Red Vienna'. At the same time, they were, until Hitler took power in Germany, oriented toward the neighboring Great Power and argued that Austria be made a part of Germany. For the Greater Germans this was the main issue; at the same time, they were anticlerical, as they regarded the power of the catholic church as an obstacle to German unification. The Christian socials, by contrast, were the voice of catholicism in Austrian politics. Tuning to the strong pro-German sentiment of the immediate postwar years, they too included a paragraph about an *Anschluss* with Germany in their program. However, it was replaced by an unambiguous allegiance to Austrian independence in their 1926 program. *Heimwehr*, the 'Catholic fascists' of Austria, echoed this in their 1930 Korneuburg Oath, where they demanded an independent *'Volksstaat der Heimwehren'*. The National Socialists that were to take over the Greater Perman Party completely were of course totally oriented toward *Anschluss* (Berchtold 1967, 235, 264, 361, 376, 402, 446; Kitchen 1980, 7-74).

The Christian socials and social democrats remained the clearly largest parties throughout the period. Almost equal in size, these parties mustered up to nearly eighty-five per cent of the vote (and close to ninety per cent of the parliamentary seats). As noted above, the support of the other nonsocialist groups, Greater Germans, *Heimatblock* or *Landbund* was enough to give the Christian social-led cabinets a majority.

In sum, France had a multiparty system based on cleavages that were more and more outdated in interwar French politics, where the left-right dimension had become dominant. Austria, by contrast, had almost a two-party system despite the fact that there were three salient cleavages in Austrian politics.

Proportional representation

The *French* Third Republic inherited its electoral system from the Second Republic. It was based on a two-ballot system with single-member constituencies; it was, in other words, a *majoritarian*, not a proportional voting system. However - and perhaps characteristically so - France does not offer an unambiguous picture in this respect, either. A new electoral law was passed in 1919 in order to advantage broad electoral alliances in the elections to the Chamber. This system was a mixture of majority and proportional electoral systems; it was applied in 1919 and again in 1924. Thereafter, however, France returned to the original voting system. All in all, therefore, France cannot be said to live up to Lijphart's requirement of proportional electoral system (Mackie and Rose 1991, 132; Hermens 1958, 274-277).

Austria, by contrast, at all times had an unambiguously proportional voting system. In fact, given her concentrated party system Austria can be regarded as one of the master cases against the thesis about an inexorable relationship between PR and the fragmentation of party systems. Between 1920 and 1923, 150 of the 165 members of the *Nationalrat* were elected from 25 constituencies with the aid of the d'Hondt highest average system. The remaining 15 seats were distributed by the same method but using the entire country as electoral district. In 1923, the d'Hondt method was replaced by the Hagenbach-Bischoff system at the constituency level. The second-stage seat distribution continued to be made using the d'Hondt system, however, now with the country divided into four groups of constituencies.

The Austrian electoral system was clearly proportional throughout the interwar period, and in fact an even greater degree of proportionality was introduced through the reforms (Mackie and Rose 1991, 23-24, 503-511; Gulick 1948, 687-691).

Territorial and nonterritorial federalism and decentralization

For centuries, *France* has been the paradigmatic case of a centralized unitary state in Europe. The Third republic entailed no change in this respect:

> The *départements* remained under the government of the Prefect, an agent and official of the central government: under him, the *Sous-Préfet* administered the *arrondissements* on the same terms of centralization (Thomson 1969, 97).

In the early 1870s, there were attempts at consolidating the regional level of French politics so as to allow a degree of decentralization. What there were of formal results of these attempts, they 'remained a dead letter' (Ibid., 98). To look for decentralization, whether territorial or nonterritorial, in interwar France is to search for a needle in a haystack where there really is none.

Austria offers quite a different picture. The constitution of 1920 declared Austria to be a federal state consisting of nine territories or *Länder*. This decision was, however, preceded by a prolonged political disagreement. The initial status of postwar Austria, as declared by the Provisional Parliament in October, 1918, was that of a centralized unitary state. After a mounting pressure from the various provinces and the nonsocialist parties that represented them, the social democrats had to agree to a federal constitution. They had, however, managed to fend off demands of fully-fledged federalism (Hoor 1966, 93-96; Graham 1924, 157-166). The constitution defined a large number of central fields where the central government held exclusive power. Besides the decisive questions of foreign, defense and customs policies, the encompassing fiscal powers of the federal parliament went to strengthen the role of the central level of government over the territories. Nevertheless, the *Länder* still retained important powers relating to, for instance, social and labor policy as well as the control of natural resources. All in all, the degree of federalism was lower than, for instance, in the United States; this notwithstanding, Austria surely fulfills the criterion of federalism and decentralization (Graham 1924, 166-167; Tingsten 1933).

In sum, the two countries are very different as concerns this dimension of Lijphart's model. France was highly centralized, whereas the Austrian state structure displayed a considerable degree of territorial federalism.

Written constitution and minority veto

'The Constitution of the Third Republic (1870-1940) was not, in reality, a constitution but a series of constitutional laws' (Hermens 1958, 264). These included a law about the organization of public authorities, including the forms guiding presidential elections. Moreover, the relations between the various governmental bodies were regulated in a special law. A third law of constitutional character determined the composition of the Senate. Electoral laws for the Chamber of Deputies as well as other laws not of strictly constitutional characters completed the constitutional framework of the Third Republic. All in all, the character of this 'Constitution' was piecemeal, and the French case hardly lives up to Lijphart's definition of 'a single document containing the basic rules of governance' (Duverger 1968, 454; Thomson 1969, 91-94).

Moreover, the French constitutional laws stipulated no strict minority veto for either constitutional revisions or other important categories of decisions. If an absolute majority in both houses was in favor of a constitutional revision, the chambers could come together as the National Assembly and adopt these changes similarly by absolute majority vote (Tingsten 1933, 133).

Again in contrast to France, *Austria* had a single written constitution. Moreover, this constitution contained clear element of a minority veto. Two thirds of the members of the lower house had to support a constitutional revision in order for this to be passed. If two thirds of the members of any of the two chambers so required, a constitutional revision must be approved by the people in a referendum. For a *total* revision of the constitution a referendum was obligatory (Graham 1924, 169-170; Gulick 1948, 843).

In sum, Austria again matched the consensus model quite well, whereas the French case lies a considerable distance away from Lijphart's description of this final dimension of the model.

France and Austria: conclusions

If France and Austria presented an enigma after the examination of party system fragmentation, the puzzle is unfortunately not smaller after these cases have been studied in the light of the consociational model. In fact, it is rather the other way around.

Clearly, as concerns the first two dimensions of the model - grand coalitions and separation of powers - none of the countries matches the consensus model. Somewhat more flexible concerning executive coalitions, France still lies some distance away from grand coalitions; in Austria, the gap between socialists and nonsocialists was never bridged by cabinet coalitions. As to the separation of powers, both countries had strongly parliament-centered systems. Interestingly enough, the French development during the Third Republic had been away from presidential power, while Austria introduced a strong presidency in 1929; the Austrian reform was, however, never put to effective practice.

As for party systems the two countries lie at approximately the same distance from the model. France had a multitude of parties, but the cleavage structure had become more and more one-dimensional. In Austria, by contrast, the number of parties was much more limited, but there were other important cleavages structuring the party system besides the left-right dimension.

The remaining three dimensions are sad reading from the point of view of the consensus model. France, the 'survivor', defies the model on every dimension, whereas Austria, the 'breakdown case' matches these dimensions quite well. Thus, Austria unlike France had a clearly proportional voting system. Moreover, France was highly centralized whereas Austria was a federal state. Finally, France had no single written constitution or a strong minority veto, while this was the case with Austria.

Evidently, the consensus model falls short of explaining the different outcomes in these two cases. A further discussion can therefore best be conducted in the following section, where all six cases included in our pairwise comparisons are surveyed together.

Consociationalism: conclusions

The main conclusion of this part of our study hardly needs to be elaborated in great detail: *what separated the 'survivors' from the three cases of 'breakdown' was not any clearcut pattern of consensus democracy* as described by Lijphart in his model. Table 9 should be sufficient to confirm this conclusion.

Table 9. Consociationalism: summary of conclusions in six cases

Country

Dimension	Cze	Fin	Fra	Lat	Est	Aust
Grand coalitions	+	(-)	(-)	-	(+)	-
Separation of pow.	+	+	(-)	-	-	(-)
Bicameralism	(+)	-	(+)	-	-	(+)
Multiparty syst.	+	+	+	+	+	(-)
Multidim. party s.	+	+	(-)	+	+	+

Proportional repr.	+	+	(-)	+	+	+
Federalism, decentr.	(-)	(+)	-	(-)	(+)	+
Written const., minority veto	+	+	-	+	+	+

Legend: Parenthesis indicate that the dimension was present but not particularly pronounced (+), or not totally absent but of little importance (-)

Czechoslovakia stands out as the consociational democracy par excellence among our six cases. Only the absence of federalism or potent decentralized structures contrasts clearly to Lijphart's model. Significantly, there was a combination of repeated executive grand coalitions and a de facto separation of powers between the executive and the legislature. Finland is the 'second best' case, although the Finnish cabinet coalitions never became grand coalitions. However, as we have argued earlier, the clear separation of governmental powers was of paramount importance in the Finnish case as well (cf. Coakley 1986, 202).

The rest of the cases - and what is worse, the rest of the dimensions - really form no meaningful pattern at all. Estonia in particular scores positively on most of Lijphart's dimensions, although a separation of powers is notably absent in this case. Most striking is the fact that the abortive democracies as a group score positively on a majority of the dimensions of consensus democracy.

Finally, the case of France remains as enigmatic as after our first empirical test. The causal background of the outcome of interwar French politics does not seem to be explicable in terms of central features of its political system.

All in all, with the exception of the Czechoslovakian case, comparative logic seems to suggest that the consociational model at large is not the key to an understanding of why democracy survived or collapsed in these cases. At the same time, we should not overlook the fact that *individual dimensions* of the model have pointed to a few rather intriguing patterns in these cases. Rather than elaborating the consensus model further, this chapter will be concluded by a discussion of these patterns.

First, there is a characteristic pattern for the introduction of the democratic constitution which seems to separate the abortive democracies from the survivors. In all three cases of 'breakdown', a radically democratic, parliament-centered constitution was introduced under strong socialist influence. In the constituent assemblies drafting the constitutions the social democrats played a leading role. They forced through a constitution which went much further in the direction of parliamentary power than most of the nonsocialist parties actually wanted. However, once the constitution went into effect, it was largely left to the nonsocialists to govern under it, whereas the socialists adopted a position of more or less permanent opposition. *Thus, those initially less attached to the constitution were left to put it into practice through executive action.*

Second, in all three cases of 'breakdown' there was an attempt - largely resisted by the social democrats - to revise the constitution so as to radically strengthen the executive. In Austria, this was actually carried through, although the process of right wing radicalization had gone so far that the reform no longer had a definite impact on the survivability of the democratic system. In the two Baltic republics, the constitutional reform was the central issue in the process which led to the collapse of democracy. The lesson would seem to be that *the strengthening of executive power in an ongoing process of polarization is a risky maneuver in a parliamentary system.*

The three 'survivors' offer a clear contrast, although a uniform pattern can by no means be found among them. In France, the decisive battles over the 1875 constitution had been fought decades ago. French parties covered a wide spectrum of ideas and policy positions, but being something else than a republican was an extreme and therefore by definition marginal posture in French interwar politics. Among the central political actors, the element of disloyal or even semiloyal opposition was rather weak.

In Czechoslovakia, the 1920 constitution was a compromise among a wide scope of Czech and Slovak actors. Moreover, the political patterns immediately after 1920 also comprised a broad cooperation of Left, Center and Right. These coalitions later carried over into cooperation across the nationalist divides as well, culminating in the grand coalitions of the 1930s.

In Finland, the social democrats had the role of a cautious bystander in the process leading to the 1919 Constitutional Act. The nonsocialists could therefore hardly claim that the constitution had been forced upon them by a powerful socialist party.

Significantly, *by the mid-1930s the social democrats had emerged as a central government party in Finland, France as well as in Czechoslovakia.* This stands i a sharp contrast to the peripheral position of the social democrats not just in Austria but largely in the two Baltic states as well.

In many ways, it appears as if the shaping of the democratic constitution had drained the collaborative potential between Left and Right in the three countries where democracy was to go under. The more gradual process of constitution-making in France and Finland and the elevated position of Masaryk as a Founding Father of Czechoslovakia apparently meant lessened political tensions connected to the constitution itself.

Chapter 5

Conclusion

This study started out with two basic assumptions. Firstly, it stressed the universal character of the interwar crisis. This called for a comparative, cross-national research strategy rather than an intensive case study. What the essential determinants of the varying outcomes of the crisis were can only be determined by systematically examining a sufficient number of cases in the light of a common set of theoretically derived explanatory factors. The truth that 'he who knows one country knows no country' is particularly acute in the context of interwar European politics.

Secondly, it was assumed that *political* factors played a central role as determinants of the fate of interwar European democracy. Without denying the importance of economic, social and cultural structures and processes, it was emphasized that the survival or breakdown of democracy concerned change and stability in constitutional and party political structures and practices. When democracy 'broke down', clear changes took place concerning the role of constitutions and political parties; they looked different and functioned differently after the 'breakdown'. Therefore, it seemed reasonable to focus on factors describing and conditioning these political structures rather than on exogeneous variables, i.e., factors in the environment of the political system. In other words, it was indeed largely assumed that 'politics explained politics' in interwar Europe.

Consequently, the present study examined number of cases, some of them well-known and well-documented, others less routinely treated in the previous literature. Most of the altogether sixteen cases represented 'survivors' from the interwar crisis, but five cases of breakdown of democracy were also included. A central notion from a theoretical point of view was that the larger and better-known countries - Germany, Italy, England and France - should not be given more weight than the smaller and less-known cases.

Two contending schools of thought furnished the study with explanatory dimensions. The starting point was what we called the *fragmentation theory*, a literature which implied a causal relationship between the degree of party system fragmentation, cabinet stability and the survivability of democracy. *Consociationalism* was the perspective which challenged this earlier theorizing; a number of dimensions culled from this theory were used systematically to describe and analyze particularly enigmatic cases.

This final chapter of the book starts out by summarizing the main findings of the study. After that, it will attempt an assessment as to how far the explanatory perspective of the study goes to explain the outcome of interwar European politics. Moreover, the remaining puzzles will be discussed in some detail and further answers to the open questions will be suggested.

Summary of findings

The analysis of the relationship between party system fragmentation, cabinet instability and the regime outcome was structured according to two different logics of inquiry present in the earlier literature. First, the sixteen cases were viewed in light of *aggregate* data using countries as units of analysis. Thereafter, *relative changes* in the degree of party system fragmentation were at the center of attention; this part of the analysis looked at time-series for each country separately. The first analysis started out from the assumption that countries at different general levels of party system fragmentation tended to have varying levels of cabinet stability, which in turn determined their capacity to manage pressures from the environment such as the Great Depression. In the 'second cut', the hypothesis was that it was the degree of change in fragmentation from one point in time to another rather than its overall level that made the crucial difference.

The aggregate-level analysis was, moreover, divided into two parts. First, bivariate statistical correlations between measures describing party systems, cabinet stability and regime outcome were examined. After that, the individual countries were placed in a matrix including all three main dimensions - level of party system fragmentation, cabinet instability and regime outcome - in order to determine to what extent the three dimensions were actually combined the way the original theory suggested.

For the aggregate-level analysis, the results could be summarized as follows:

1 The survival or breakdown of democracy does not appear to be explicable in terms of bivariate statistical relationships between party system characteristics and the ultimate fate of democracy.

2 By contrast, cabinet duration seems to offer a statistically significant explanation of the breakdown or survival of democracy; cabinet instability in these terms appears to be a necessary but not a sufficient condition for the breakdown of democracy.

3 The fragmentation of the party system is to some extent related to cabinet instability; these relationships are, however, not statistically significant.

4 'Polarized fragmentation' and the relative fragmentation of the socialist and nonsocialist wings do not constitute adequate explanations of either the breakdown of democracy or the degree of cabinet instability.

5 When the median values of the main explanatory dimensions (fragmentation and instability) are combined, roughly half of the cases comply with the suppositions of the original theory.

As for the analysis of relative changes within individual countries, the following conclusions could be drawn:

1 Cabinet stability went from low to very low immediately prior to the breakdown of democracy.

2 There is no 'critical threshold' of party system fragmentation above which increases in fragmentation lead to clear increases in cabinet or constitutional instability.

3 Relative changes in party systemic factors possess limited explanatory power vis-à-vis political stability. They more frequently coincide with changes in stability in those countries where democracy survived than in those where

democracy went under.

Taken together, these analyses produced the following general conclusions:

All five cases of 'breakdown' were generally unstable democracies, and their cabinet stability decreased immediately prior to the collapse of democratic rule. Four of the five cases had generally high levels of party system fragmentation. Indeed, they were 'paradigmatic cases' through the combination of party system fragmentation, low cabinet stability and the eventual breakdown of democracy.

All cases of generally high cabinet stability were among the 'survivors' among interwar European democracies. In other words, the interwar crisis did not destabilize previously stable regimes to a decisive degree. Indeed, as Linz has pointed out (1978, 5-8), 'stability bred stability' in Europe between the world wars. Save for one country (Austria), all cases of generally low party system fragmentation were among the 'survivors'. A majority of them combined low fragmentation with high levels of cabinet stability.

The second main part of the empirical analysis consisted of three pairwise case studies: Czechoslovakia was compared to Latvia, Finland to Estonia and France to Austria. In each pair, the first country was a 'survivor' and the second an abortive democracy. The two first pairs - Czechoslovakia-Latvia and Finland-Estonia could be said to represent 'most similar cases', whereas France and Austria differed in most respects except the fact that both countries displayed high cabinet instability.

The comparison was based on the eight dimensions of Arend Lijphart's model of 'consensus democracy'. In the analysis itself, two of the dimensions - 'multiparty system' and 'multidimensional party system' - were treated under the same heading. Apart from this, the comparative case studies were structured according to Lijphart's model. The results were far from promising from the point of view of the model.

What separated the 'survivors' from the three cases of 'breakdown' was not any clearcut pattern of consensus democracy as described by Lijphart in his model. In fact, taken together the three 'survivors' matched the dimensions of the consensus model just as insufficiently as thre three cases where democracy broke down.

Czechoslovakia stood out as the clearest case of consensus democracy, although it did lack the kinds of federalistic or decentralizing structures that the model presumed. Finland was an intermediate case, whereas France defied the model on almost all points. What was perhaps even more disheartening from the point of view of the model was the fact that the three cases of 'breakdown' displayed several, although by no means all of the characteristic features of the consensus model.

Evidently, consociationalism as such was not the key to the survivability of European democracy at large. All the same, individual dimensions of the model pointed to some intriguing patterns. The *introduction of the democratic constitution* as such seemed to be a dividing line: in Latvia, Estonia asd particularly in Austria the coalition which established the radically democratic constitution split directly after its introduction, leaving the nonsocialists, who were largely uneasy about the extremely parliamentary form of government, in charge of its management. In Czechoslovakia, the comprehensive consensus about the constitution almost always guaranteed substantial majority cabinets, even a number of grand coalitions. In Finland, the peripheral position of the Left in the 1919 constitutional process meant that the form of government lacked the 'leftist image' typical of the hyperparliamentary democracies. In France, the fundamental disagreements over the republican constitution had been overcome well before the World War.

Furthermore, in all three cases of breakdown there was an *attempt to strengthen the executive at the expense of the parliament*. This attempt was immediately linked to the process which led to the breakdown of democracy in Latvia and Estonia. In Austria, it marked the beginning of the definite polarization which led to the demise of democratic rule. In all three cases, the social democrats resisted this attempt while most of the nonsocialist parties supported the reform.

In the three successful democracies, by contrast, the relationship between the executive and the parliament was stable throughout the period. Finland in particular offers a contrast to its counterpart Estonia: the strong presidency provided by the 1919 Finnish constitution helped the government manage the acute crisis in the early 1930s successfully. Also in Czechoslovakia, the de facto separation of powers functioned as an instrument of consensus among the nationalities as well as between Left and Right.

Finally, *by the mid-1930s the social democrats had emerged as a central government party in Finland, France as well as in Czechoslovakia.* This stood in a clear contrast to Austria in particular; the peripheral role of the social democrats in Estonia and Latvia reinforces this contrast as well.

In sum, it was not consociationalism as a fully-fledged system that made the difference. Cases of 'breakdown' displayed many of Lijphart's dimensions, while one successful democracy (France) almost completely lacked such characteristics. More significantly, the analysis directs the attention to the process and timing of constitution-making and constitutional reform. Clearly, the historical aspects of democratic rule seem to be of importance for the viability of interwar European democracy. This links our analysis back to the historical narratives in Chapter 2. The following section reflects upon the connection between our two systematic analyses and these historical aspcets at some length.

Reflections

The concluding discussion in connection with Chapter 2 pointed to the well-known difference in political outcome between the early and late democratizers among European nations. Overall, a gradual and early introduction of democratic institutions predestined for viable democracy, whereas the majority of states where democracy appeared late and suddenly faced great difficulties in the interwar period. The successor states of World War I as well as Germany and Austria belonged to this groups of states.

In this respect, the successful democracies of Czechoslovakia and Finland would appear to be exceptions that are difficult to account for. Certainly, the settlement in connection with the collapse of the Habsburg and Russian empires, respectively, would seem to have entailed the most dramatic discontinuity in political institutions. Similarly, Czechoslovakia and Finland like Austria, Germany and the Baltic states introduced new democratic constitutions in the wake of the World War.

Still, we would argue that the cases of Czechoslovakia and Finland, although certainly different from cases of more continuous and gradual democratization in Western and Northwestern Europe, differ from the other 'new' democracies by their greater degree of political continuity. There was a greater degree of continuity between prewar politics and the constitutional settlement of the immediate postwar era. There was, moreover, a greater degree of political continuity between the coalitions which drafted the constitutions and the coalitions that became dominant in interwar executive politics in these two countries.

The *Reichsrat* of the Austrian part of the Habsburg Monarchy was arranged on a democratic basis in 1907. Although democracy suffered several setbacks prior to the World War, the Czechs and Slovaks (who together with the other Slavic groups held the majority) were able to form modern democratic parties during this period. Most significantly, the Czecho-Slovak National Committee, which adopted the Constitution of independent Czechoslovakia, was structured according to the strength that the major Czech parties had gained in the 1911 Reichsrat elections; to these parties, Slovak representatives were added. Thus, as Coakley (1986, 194) has aptly pointed out, the National Committee was a 'conservative body' rather than a revolutionary coalition.

By the same token, the continuity from the Czecho-Slovak National Committee to interwar politics in Czechoslovakia was considerable. The Czech coalitions that ruled in the first part of the 1920s were basically a continuation of the political pattern of the National Committee. The bulk of the parties represented in these cabinets continued in the excecutive as it later developed toward genuine grand coalitions comprising German parties as well. Parties and political leaders active in the Reichsrat and the National Committee played significant roles in interwar coalitions as well. Czechoslovak politics were characterized by change and reform, but there was no dramatic rupture with the principles and practices of the past.

Similarly, despite the tragic and divisive Civil War of 1918, the Finnish political system of the early 1920s bore a surprisingly strong mark of continuity and compromise. Both Left, Center and Right could claim to have won important victories in the constitutional settlements; no-one won an all-out victory, no-one lost everything. The Left and the Center managed to safeguard the position of the parliament in the government machinery; the 1906 Representative Reform was for all practical purpose kept in force. This is to say that the right wing had to reconciliate itself to an institution which it had viewed with profound suspicion. Moreover, the Right had to give up its dream of a monarchy. But, and this is a crucial qualification, the constitutional defeat of the Right was far from complete. The influence of the parliament was balanced by a strong presidency, and this institution can largely be seen as a compensation to the Right for the failure to establish a monarchy.

The 1919 constitutional settlement in Finland was far from 'revolutionary'. The imprint left by the socialists was rather weak; the settlement was largely an affair between Center and Right. Similarly, these groups came to be dominant in cabinet politics throughout the 1920s and early 1930s. Nevertheless, the social democrats were part and parcel of the normal democratic process. The fact that they were able to form a minority cabinet in 1926 (and keep it alive for over a year) indicates that they were anything but totally marginalized in Finnish politics.

The 'revolutionary' character of the new constitutions in the Baltic countries, Austria and Germany stands in a contrast to the more 'conservative' character of the settlements in Czechoslovakia and Finland. In the Baltic countries, the previous democratic experience of the political elites, let alone of the population at large, was minimal. In Germany and Austria, steps toward mass democracy had certainly occurred before the world war; the political and constitutional discontinuity from the prewar years to the constitutional settlement after the war was nevertheless marked. In Germany, the Right was alienated from the political system created in 1919. In the Baltic countries and in Austria, the nonsocialist parties governed under constitutions which to a large extent bore the imprint of the social democrats. There was a double discontinuity: the constitutions had next to no roots in earlier political structures, and the governing coalitions were not those that had introduced the constitutions.

Correspondingly, the French case can best be understood in terms of constitutional and institutional continuity. Party system fragmentation and cabinet instability complicated the management of political issues, but they did not place the democratic system as such at risk; the foundations of the democratic system had been established long before the interwar era, and the main political groups and actors had clearly invested their loyalties in the Republic. The interwar era did not entail either new fundamental issues or new constellations of political forces or government coalitions. At times of crisis all major political groups hurried to the rescue of the Republic. Loyalty to the sitting cabinet was never to be taken for granted; loyalty to the Republic was a *conditio sine qua non* in French politics.

These reflections should not be interpreted in the favor of historical determinism: not all radically new constitutions and coalitions are moribund, not all cases of constitutional continuity (Italy is a case in point) display successful democracy. But as in many other walks of life, those who were lucky yesterday are likely to be lucky today as well. The countries which had the opportunity to fight the decisive battles over democracy and parliamentarism long before the end of the war were in a radically better position than those in which democratization started and ended with the postwar constitutional settlement. The fragmentation of party systems was a complicating factor from the point of view of the stability of democracy; if democracy had sufficiently deep roots it needed not be a deadly threat. Executive instability naturally created pressures on the survivability of the democratic system itself. However, its effects were much more devastating if large segments of the political field were disloyal or semiloyal to the democratic institutions themselves. Consociational arrangements and practices were conducive to the viability of democratic rule. Consociationalism in itself was, however, more an effect of early democratic consensus than a cause of the establishment of a stable democracy.

Bibliography

Aarebrot, F. 1991, 'Dutch Democracy in the Inter-War Period. A Research Note', *Paper Presented at the Meeting of the Research Group on Crisis, Compromise, Collapse - Conditions for Democracy in Inter-War Europe, Budapest, January 24th-27th, 1991*.

Adamthwaite, A. 1977, *France and the Coming of the Second World War 1936-1939*, London: Frank Cass.

Alapuro, R. 1988, *State and Revolution in Finland*, Berkeley: University of California Press.

Allum, P.A. 1973, *Italy - Republic without Government?*, London: Weidenfeld.

Anckar, D. 1990, 'Democracy in Finland: The Constitutional Framework', in J. Sundberg and S. Berglund, eds., *Finnish Democracy*, Jyväskylä 1990: The Finnish Political Science Association, 26-50.

Anckar, D. 1987, 'Finlands presidentmakt', in U. Lindström and L. Karvonen, eds., *Finland. En politisk loggbok*, Stockholm: Almqvist & Wiksell International, 57-92.

Andics, H. 1984, *Der Staat, den keiner wollte. Österreich von der Gründung der Republik bis zur Moskauer Deklaration*, Wien: Wilhelm Goldmann Verlag.

Arntzen, J.G. and B.B. Knudsen 1981, *Political Life and Institutions in Norway*, Oslo: University of Oslo.

Baglieri, J. 1980, 'Italian Fascism and the Crisis of Liberal Hegemony: 1901-1922', in S.U. Larsen, B. Hagtvet and J.P. Myklebust, eds., *Who Were the Fascists. Social Roots of European Fascism*, Bergen - Oslo - Tromsö: Universitetsforlaget, 318-336.

Balodis, A. 1990, *Lettlands och det lettiska folkets historia*, Stockholm: Lettiska Nationella Fonden.

Barr Carson, G., ed., 1956, 'Latvia: An Area Study. Volume II', *Subcontractors Monograph. Printed by Human Relations Microfilms*, Yale Station, New Haven, Connecticut.

Bentley, M. 1985, *Politics without Democracy. Great Britain 1815-1914*, Totowa, N.J.: Barnes and Noble Books.

Berchtold, K. 1967, Hrsgb., *Österreichische Parteiprogramme 1868-1966*, Wien: Verlag für Geschichte und Politik.

Berglund, S. and U. Lindström 1978, *The Scandinavian Party System(s)*, Lund: Studentlitteratur.

Berg-Schlosser, D. 1990, 'Multi-case analysis - the "missing link" between configurative and macro-quantitative approaches', *Paper to be presented at the session of the Reserach Committee on Comparative Sociology on 'Comparative Sociology: Theory, Method, Substance' at the occasion of the XIIth World Congress of Sociology, Madrid, July 9-13, 1990*.

Bilmanis, A. 1934, *Latvijas Werdegang. Vom Bischofsstaat Terra Mariana bis zur freien Volksrepublik*, Leipzig: Bernhard Lamey Verlag.

Botz, G. 1980, 'Intröduction', in S.U. Larsen, B. Hagtvet and J.P. Myklebust, eds., *Who Were the Fascists. Social Roots of European Fascism*, Bergen - Oslo - Tromsö: Universitetsforlaget, 192-201.

Browne, E., J. Frendeis, and D. Gleiber 1986, 'Dissolution of Governments in Scandinavia: A Critical Events Perspective', *Scandinavian Political Studies*, Vol. 9 , 93-110.

Bruegel, J.W. 1973, *Czechoslovakia before Munich. The German Minority Problem and British Appeasement Policy*, London: Cambridge at the University Press.

Burian, P. 1967, 'Demokratie und Parlamentarismus in der Ersten Tschechoslowakischen Republik', in H-E. Volkmann, Hrsgb., *Die Krise des Parlamentarismus in Ostmitteleuropa zwischen den beiden Weltkriegen*, Marburg/Lahn: J.G. Herder-Institut, 85-102.

Coakley, J. 1986, 'Political succession and regime change in new states in inter-war Europe: Ireland, Finland, Czechoslovakia and the Baltic Republics', *European Journal of Political Reesearch*, 14, 1986, 187-206.

Codding, G.A. 1965, *The Federal Government of Switzerland*, Boston: Houghton Miffin Company.

Cole, A. and P. Campbell 1989, *French Electoral Systems and Elections Since 1789*, Aldershot: Gower.

Conze, W. 1964, *Die Zeit Wilhelms II und die Weimarer Republik. Deutsche Geschichte 1890-1933*, Tübingen: Rainer Wunderlich Verlag.

Craig, G. 1978, *Germany 1866-1945*, Oxford: Clarendon Press.

De Meur, G. and D. Berg-Schlosser 1990, 'Crisis and Compromise in Belgium in the Inter-War Period, *Paper Presented at a Conference on the Conditions for Democracy in Interwar Europe*, Madrid July 9-13 , 1990.

Dobry, M. 1989, 'Février 1934 et la découverte d l'allergie de la société francaise à la "Révolution fasciste"', *Révue francaise de sociologie* XXX, 1989, 511-533.

Dodd, L. 1976, *Coalitions in Parliamentary Government*, Princeton, N.J.: Princeton University Press.

Dogan, M. 1989, 'Irremovable Leaders and Ministerial Instability in European Democracies', in M. Dogan, ed., *Pathways to Power. Selecting Rulers in Pluralist Democracies*, Boulder, Colorado: Westview Press.

Downs, A. 1957, *An Economic Theory of Democracy*, New York: Harper and Row.

Duverger, M. 1968, *Institutions politiques et droit constitutionnel*, Paris: Presses Universitaires de France.

Duverger, M. 1951, *Les partis politiques*, Paris: Librairie Armand Colin.

Eckstein, H. 1968, 'Parties, political: Party Systems', in D.L. Sills, ed., *International Encyclopedia of the Social Sciences, Vol. 11*, USA: The Macmillan Company & The Free Presss, 436-453.

Eichengreen, B. and T.J. Hatton 1988, 'Interwar Unemployment in International Perspective: An Overview', in B. Eichengreen and T.J. Hatton, eds., *Interwar Unemployment in International Perspective*, Dodrecht: Kluwer Academic Publishers, 1-60.

Fritsche, P. 1987, *Die politische Kultur Italiens*, Frankfurt: Campus Verlag.

Furre, B. 1972, *Norsk historie 1905-1940*, Oslo: Det Norske Samlaget.

Garleff, M. 1978, 'Ethnic Minorities in the Estonian and Latvian Parliaments: The Politics of Coalition', in V.S. Vardys and R. Misiunas, eds., *The Baltic States in Peace and War 1917-1945*, University Park: Pennsylvania State University Press, 81-94.

Garraty, J.A. 1986, *The Great Depresssion*, New York: Harcourt, Brace & Jovanovich.

Gladdish, K. 1991, *Governing from the Centre: Politics and Policy-Making in the Netherlands*, London: Hurst & Co.

Glaus, B. 1980, 'The National Front in Switzerland', in S.U. Larsen, B. Hagtvet and J.P. Myklebust, eds., *Who Were the Fascists. Social Roots of European Fascism*, Bergen -Oslo - Tromsö: Universitetsforlaget, 467-

478.

Goossens, M., S. Peeters and G. Pepermans 1988, 'Interwar Unemployment in Belgium', in Eichengreen and T.J. Hatton, eds., *Interwar Unemployment in International Perspective*, Dordrecht: Kluwer Academic Publishers, 289-324.

Goudsblom, J. 1967, *Dutch Society*, New York: Random House.

Gourevitch, P. A. 1986, *Politics in Hard Times: Comparative Responses to International Crisis*, Ithaca: Cornell University Press.

Graham, M.W. 1924, *New Governments of Central Europe*, New York: Henry Holt and Company.

Greene, N. 1970, *From Versailles to Vichy. The Third Republic 1919-1940*, Arlington Height, Illinois: AHM Publishers.

Gulick, C.A. 1948, *Austria from Habsburg to Hitler*, Berkeley: University of California Press.

Hämäläinen, P.K. 1966, *The Nationality Struggle between the Finns and the Swedish-Speaking Minority in Finland*, Bloomington, Indiana: Indiana University Press.

Hapala, M. E. 1968, 'Political Parties in Czechoslovakia, 1918-1938', in M. Rechcigl, Jr., ed., *Czechoslovakia Past and Present. Volume I. Political, International, Social and Economic Aspects*, The Hague: Mouton, 124-140.

Helander, V. 1976, 'Kamari vai kirjaamo. Eduskunnan suuri valiokunta Suomen lainsäädäntöjärjestelmän osana vuosina 1907-1971', *Turun yliopiston politiikan tutkimuksen ja sosiologian laitos. Valtio-opillisia tutkimuksia N:o 32*.

Hermens, F. 1941, *Democracy or Anarchy? A Study of Proportional Representation*, Notre Dame, Ind.: The University of Notre Dame Press.

Hermens, F. 1951, *Europe Under Democracy or Anarchy*, Notre Dame, Ind.: The University of Notre Dame Press.

Hermens, F. 1958, *The Representative Republic*, Notre Dame, Ind.: The University of Notre Dame Press.

Höjer, C-H. 1946, *Le régime parlementaire belge de 1918 à 1940*, Uppsala: Almqvist & Wiksell.

Hoor, E. 1966, *Österreich 1918-1938. Staat ohne Nation. Republik ohne Republikaner*, Wien: Österreichischer Bundesverlag für Unterricht,

Wissenschaft und Kunst.

Jääskeläinen, M. 1977, 'Keskustapolitiikan aika'; 'Porvarilliset kokoomushallitukset'; 'Vähemmistöhallitukset'; 'Demokratian kriisi'; 'Keskustan ja vasemmiston yhteistyö', in *Valtioneuvoston historia 1917-1966, I*, Helsinki: Valtioneuvoston historiakomitea, 273-618.

Jackson, J. 1988, *The Popular Front in France defending democracy, 1934-38*, Cambridge: Cambridge University Press.

Jungar, A-C. 1991, 'Italian Socialism: A Century of Trial and Error', in L. Karvonen and J. Sundberg, eds., *Social Democracy in Transition. Northern, Southern and Eastern Europe*, Aldershot: Dartmouth, 243-268.

Karvonen, L. 1989, 'Against the Odds. The Crisis of Finnish Democracy in the Inter-War Period', *Working paper prepared for the Conference 'The Search for Stability in Europe: Social Change & Economic Policy in the 1930s', Oxford 9-12 November, 1989.*

Karvonen, L. 1991 A, '"A Nation of Workers and Peasants". Ideology and Compromise in the Interwar Years', in L. Karvonen and J. Sundberg, eds., *Social Democracy in Transition. Northern, Southern and Eastern Europe*, Aldershot: Dartmouth, 49-82.

Karvonen, L. 1988, *From White to Blue-and-Black. Finnish Fascism in the Inter-War Era*, Helsinki: Societas Scientarum Fennica.

Karvonen, L. 1991 B, 'Oikeistoradikalismin loppunäytös: Mäntsälän kapinasta Isänmaalliseen kansanliikkeeseen' *Politiikka* 2/1991, 106-115.

Karvonen, L. and U. Lindström 1988, 'Red-Green Crisis Agreements: The Great Depression in Scandinavia in a Comparative Perspective', *Paper Prepared for Presentation at the XIVth World Congress of the International Political Science Association, Washington, D.C., August through September 1, 1988.*

Kastari, P. 1969, 'The Position of the President in the Finnish Political System', *Scandinavian Political Studies*, Vol. 4, 1969, 151-159.

Key, V.O. 1959, *Politics, Parties and Pressure Groups*, New York: Thomas Y. Cromwell.

Kitchen, M. 1980, *The Coming of Austrian Fascism*, London: Croom Helm.

Koch, H.W. 1984, *A Constitutional History of Germany in the Nineteenth and Twentieth Centuries*, London: Longman.

180 FRAGMENTATION AND CONSENSUS

Kühnl, R. 1985, *Die Weimarer Republik*, Reinbek bei Hamburg: Rowohlt.

Lemberg, H. 1967, 'Gefahrenmomente für die demokratische Staatsform der Ersten Tschechoslowakischen Republik', in H-E. Volkmann, Hrsgb., *Die Krise des Parlamentarismus in Ostmitteleuropa zwischen den beiden Weltkriegen*, Marburg/Lahn: J.G. Herder-Institut, 103-120.

Lewin, L. 1984, *Ideologi och struktur. Svensk politik under 100 år*, Stockholm: P.A. Norstedt & Söners Förlag.

Lijphart, A. 1984, *Democracies. Patterns of Majoritarian and Consensus Government in Twenty-One Countries*, New Haven: Yale University Press.

Lijphart, A. 1977, *Democracy in Plural Societies. A Comparative Exploration*, New Haven: Yale University Press.

Lindström, U. 1985, *Fascism in Scandinavia 1920-1940*, Lund: Studentlitteratur.

Linz, J. J. 1991, 'La crisis de las democracias', in M. Cabrera, S. Juliá & P.M. Aceña, comps., *Europa en crisis*, Madrid: Editorial Pablo Iglesias.

Linz, J. J. 1980, 'Political Space and Fascism as a Late-Comer: Conditions Conducive to the Success or Failure of Fascism as a Mass Movement in Inter-War Europe', in S.U. Larsen, B. Hagtvet and J.P. Myklebust, eds., *Who Were the Fascists. Social Roots of European Fascism*, Bergen - Oslo- Tromsö: Universitetsforlaget, 153-191.

Linz, J.J. 1987, *The Breakdown of Democratic Regimes. Crisis, Breakdown & Reequilibration*, Baltimor: The Johns Hopkins University Press.

Lipset, S.M. 1981, *Political Man. The Social Bases of Politics*, Baltimore: The Johns Hopkins University Press.

Luebbert, G. 1991, *Liberalism, Fascism, or Social Democracy. Social Classes and the Political Origins of Regimes in Interwar Europe*, New York: Oxford University Press.

Mackie, T. and R. Rose 1974, *The International Almanac of Electoral History*, London: Macmillan.

Mackie, T. and R. Rose 1991, *The International Almanac of Electoral History*, London: Macmillan.

Mägi, Artur 1967, *Das Staatsleben Estlands während seiner Selbständigkeit. I. Das Regierungssystem*, Stockholm: Almqvist & Wiksell.

Manning, M. 1970, *The Blueshirts*, Dublin: Gill and Macmillan.

Mayer, L. 1980 A, 'A Note on the Aggregation of Party Systems', in P. Merkl, ed., *Western European Party Systems. Trends and Prospects*, New York: The Free Press, 515-520.

Mayer, L. 1980 B, 'Party Systems and Cabinet Stability', in P. Merkl, ed., *Western European Party Systems. Trends and Prospects*, New York: The Free Press, 335-347.

Mayer, L. 1989, *Redefining Comparative Politics. Promise Versus Performance*, Newbury Park: SAGE Publications.

McMillan, J. 1985, *Dreyfus to De Gaulle. Politics and Society in France 1898-1969*, London: Edward Arnold.

Merkl, P. 1980, 'Comparing Fascist Movements', in S.U. Larsen, B. Hagtvet and J.P. Myklebust, eds., *Who Were the Fascists. Social Roots of European Fascism*, Bergen - Oslo - Tromsö: Universitetsforlaget, 752-783.

Miller, K. E. 1991, *Denmark. A Troubled Welfare State*, Boulder, Colorado: Westview Press.

Mlynarik, J. 1989, 'The Nationality Question in Czechoslovakia and the 1938 Munich Agreement', in N. Stone and E. Strohal, eds., *Czechoslovakia: Crossroads and Crises, 1918-88*, Basingstoke: Macmillan, 89-100.

Mohlin, Y. 1987, 'Finlands inbördeskrig', in U. Lindström and L. Karvonen, eds., *Finland. En politisk loggbok*, Stockholm: Almqvist & Wiksell International, 9-56.

Mohlin, Y. 1991, *Från demokrati till diktatur. Central- och Östeuropa under mellankrigstiden*, Lund: Studentlitteratur.

Myklebust, J-P. and S. Ugelvik Larsen 1980, 'Regional Contrasts in the Membership Base of the Nasjonal Samling', in S. Ugelvik Larsen, B. Hagtvet and J-P. Myklebust, eds., *Who Were the Fascists. Social Roots of European Fascism*, Bergen - Oslo - Tromsö: Universitetsforlaget, 621-650.

Newman, K.J. 1970, *European Democracy Between the Wars*, London: George Allen & Unwin Ltd.

Nicholls, A.J. 1985, *Weimar and the Rise of Hitler*, London: Macmillan.

Nolte, E. 1968, *De fascistiska rörelserna*, Stockholm: Bokförlaget Aldus/Bonniers.

Nousiainen, J. 1971, *The Finnish Political System*, Cambridge, Massachusetts:

Harvard University Press.

Pachter, H.M. 1978, *Modern Germany. A Social, Cultural and Political History*, Boulder, Colorado: Westview Press.

Parming, T. 1975, *The Collapse of Liberal Democracy and the Rise of Authritarianism in Estonia*, London: SAGE Publications.

Pauley, B. F. 1980, 'Nazis and Heimwehr Fascists: the Struggle for Supremacy in Austria, 1918-1938', in S.U. Larsen, B. Hagtvet and J.P. Myklebust, eds., *Who Were the Fascists. Social Roots of European Fascism*, Bergen - Oslo - Tromsö: Universitetsforlaget, 226-238..

Prager, J. 1986, *Building Democracy in Ireland. Political Order in a Newly Independent Nation*, Cambridge: Cambridge University Press.

Przeworski, A. and H. Teune 1970, *The Logic of Comparative Social Inquiry*, New York: Wiley-Interscience.

Pugh, M. 1985, *The Making of Modern British Politics 1867-1939*, London: Basil Blackwell.

Rath, J. and C.W. Schum 1980, 'The Dollfuss Regime: Fascist or Authoritarian?', in S.U. Larsen, B. Hagtvet and J.P. Myklebust, eds., *Who Were the Fascists. Social Roots of European Fascism*, Bergen - Oslo - Tromsö: Universitetsforlaget, 249-257.

von Rauch, G. 1974, *The Baltic States. The Years of Independence. Estonia, Latvia, Lithuania 1917-1940*, Berkeley: University of California Press.

Raun, T.U. 1987, *Estonia and the Estonians*, Stanford, California: Hoover Institution Press, Stanford University.

Regenten und Regierungen der Welt. Teil II: 1492-1953, Bearbeitet von Bertold Spuler, herausgegeben von A.G. Ploetz, Bielefeld 1953.

Rémond, R. 1969, *The Right Wing in France from 1815 to De Gaulle*, Philadeplhia: University of Pennsylvania Press.

Rintala, M. 1962, *Three Generations. The Extreme Right Wing in Finnish Politics*, Bloomington, Indiana: The University of Indiana Press.

Ruffieux, R. 1983, 'Les données de l'histoire constitutionnelle', in A. Riklin, ed., *Manuel du system politique de la Suisse. Vol. I: le Contexte*, Bern: Paul Haupt Verlag.

Rumpf, E. 1959, *Nationalismus und Sozialismus in Irland*, Meisenheim an Glan: Verlag Anton Hain K.G.

Rundle, S. 1946, *Language as a Social and Political Factor in Europe*,

London: Faber and Faber Limited.

Ryssevik, J. 1991, 'Party vs. Parliament. Contrasting Configurations of Electoral and Ministerial Socialism in Scandinavia', in L. Karvonen and J. Sundberg, eds., *Social Democracy in Transition. Northern, Southern and Eastern Europe*, Aldershot: Dartmouth, 15-48.

Sani G. and G. Sartori 1985, 'Polarization, Fragmentation and Competition in Western Democracies', in H. Daalder and P. Mair, eds., *Western European Party Systems. Continuity and Change*, Beverly Hills - London - New Delhi: Sage Publications, 307-340.

Sartori, G. 1990, 'A Typology of Party Systems', in P. Mair, ed., *The West European Party System*, Oxford: Oxford University Press, 317-349.

Sartori, G. 1991, 'Comparing and Miscomparing', *Journal of Theoretical Politics*, Vol. 3, Number 3, July 1991, 243-257.

Sartori, G. 1987, *The Theory of Democracy Revisited. Part One: The Contemporary Debate*, New Jersey: Chatham House Publishers.

Schephens, L. 1980, 'Fascists and Nationalists in Belgium, 1919-1940, in S.U. Larsen, B. Hagtvet and J.P. Myklebust, eds., *Who Were the Fascists. Social Roots of European Fascism*, Bergen - Oslo - Tromsö: Universitetsforlaget.

Silde, A. 1976, *Latvijas vesture 1914-1940. Valsts tapsana un suverena valsts*, Daugava: AD.

Spekke, A. 1951, *History of Latvia. An Outline*, Stockholm: M. Goppers.

Stjernquist, N. 1966, 'Sweden: Stability or Deadlock?', in R.A. Dahl, ed., *Political Opposition in Western Democracies*, New Haven: Yale University Press, 116-146.

Stephens, J.D. 1989, ' Democratic Transition and Breakdown in Western Europe, 1870-1939: A Test of the Moore Thesis', *American Journal of Sociology*, Vol. 94, Number 5 (March 1989), 1019-1077.

Stone, N. 1989, 'Introductory Essay: Czechoslovakia', in N. Stone and E. Strouhal, eds., *Czechoslovakia: Crossroads and Crises, 1918-1989*, Basingstoke: Macmillan, 1-10.

Svabe, A. 1961, *Lettlands historia*, Stockholm: Lettiska Nationella Fonden.

Svensson, P. 1986, 'Stability, Crisis and Breakdown: Some Notes on the Concept of Crisis in Political Analysis', *Scandinavian Political Studies*, Vol. 9 - No. 2, 1986, 129-139.

Taagepera, R. and M. Soberg Shugart 1989, *Seats and Votes. The Effects & Determinants of Electoral Systems*, New Haven: Yale University Press.

Táborsky, E. 1968, 'The Roots of Czechoslovak Democracy', in M. Rechcigl, Jr., ed., *Czechoslovakia Past and Present. Volume I. Political, International, Social, and Economic Aspects*, The Hague: Mouton, 117-123.

Taylor, A.J.P. 1966, *English History 1914-1945*, Oxford: The Clarendon Press.

Taylor, M. and V. Herman 1971, 'Party Systems and Government Stability', *American Political Science Review* 65, 28-37.

Thomson, D. 1969, *Democracy in France since 1870*, London: Oxford University Press.

Tiersky, R. 1974, *French Communism, 1920-1972*, New York: Columbia University Press.

Tingsten, H. 1933, *Demokratiens seger och kris. Den författningspolitiska utvecklingen 1880-1930*, Stockholm: Albert Bonniers Förlag.

Tingsten, H. 1936, *Den nationella diktaturen. Nazismens och fascismens idéer*, Stockholm: Albert Bonniers Förlag.

Tingsten, H. 1930, *Från parlamentarism till diktatur. Fascismens erövring av Italien*, Stockholm: Bokförlaget Natur och Kultur.

Vardys, V.S. 1978, 'The Rise of Authoritarian Rule in the Baltic States', in V.S. Vardys and R.J. Misiunas, eds., *The Baltic States in Peace and War 1917-1945*, University Park: Pennsylvania State University Press, 65-80.

Weiss, H. 1967, 'Baltische Nationalitätenprobleme und Parlamentarismus', in H-E. Volkmann, Hrsgb., *Die Krise des Parlamentarismus in Ostmitteleuropa zwischen den beiden Weltkriegen*, Marburg/Lahn: J.G. Herder-Institut, 168-176.

Wiberg, M. 1988, *Between Apathy and Revolution: Explications of the Conditions for Political Legitimacy*, Turku: Annales Universitatis Turkuensis.

van der Wusten, H. and R.E. Smit 1980, 'Dynamics of the Dutch National Socialist Movement (the NSB): 1931-1935', in S.U. Larsen, B. Hagtvet and J.P. Myklebust, eds., *Who Were the Fascists. Social Roots of European fascism*, Bergen - Oslo - Tromsö: Universitetsforlaget.

Zimmermann, E. 1988, 'The Puzzle of Government Duration. Evidence from

Six European Countries during the Interwar Period', *Comparative Politics* Vol. 20, 341-357.

Zimmermann, E. and T. Saalfeld 1988, 'Economic and Political Reactions to the World Economic Crisis of the 1930s in Six European Countries', *International Studies Quarterly* (1988), 32, 305-334.